ECONOMIC JUSTICE IN ISLAM

BY

Dr S. M. YUSUF

Professor of Arabic, Department of Religious Studies
University of Jos (Nigeria)

KITAB BHAVAN
New Delhi-110002

KITAB BHAVAN
Publishers, Distributors, Exporters & Importers
1784, Kalan Mahal, Darya Ganj,
New Delhi - 1100 02 (India)

Phones : (91-11) 23277392 / 93,
23274686, 32906494
Fax : (91-11) 23263383
Website : www.kitabbhavan.com
Email : nasri@vsnl.com
: nusrat@bol.net.in

First Published in Inida ... 1988
2nd Edition 2009

ISBN : 81-7151-036-1
Book Code No. : E00023

Printed & Published in India by :
Nusrat Ali Nasri for KITAB BHAVAN
1784, Kalan Mahal, Darya Ganj,
New Delhi - 1100 02 [India]

PREFACE

The capitalist system of economy plagued the Muslim countries as part of the Western civilisation which engulfed them in the wake of their political subjugation. The Muslims singled out the most palpable feature of it, namely, the *ribā*, for severe condemnation, which was but due from the Islamic viewpoint. However, the Muslim scholarship, being at a low ebb, failed to make a comprehensive and penetrating study of the entire capitalistic system of economy so as to evalute and expose the other features of it which, through a dialectical process, developed in its womb the ideology of socialism and gave birth to the system of totalitarian economy run by a powerful junta in the name of the revengeful dictatorship of the proletariat.

Since the rise of socialism Islam has been on the defensive. The defence is based primarily on religious faith, which is unwittingly designated by the fashionable unreligious term "ideology". The defenders would not concern themselves with an appeal to reason in relation to the actual problems of this mundane world. For long no serious attention was paid to reconstructing the Islamic system of economy and presenting it in an intelligible way to the modern world. An unfortunate result of this exclusive concern with ideology is the identification of Islam with the props of a crumbling, intolerably unjust economic order.

Iqbal was the first to proclaim that the rise of socialism was Islam's opportunity—an opportunity for Islam to rediscover itself and to project itself so as to pose a challenge to socialism while making the best of the decay of capitalism. It called for a revolution within the Islamic society before Islam set about to revolutionise the world. That was not to be.

The tyranny of landlordism continued to rage unabated in the Muslim lands. The banking, commercial and industrial systems of the West became the order of the day with the support of the ruling class and the big business despite the condemnation of *ribā* by the religious doctors and the common people. With political independence, industrialism emerged as the prime policy of the State. Soon the phenomenon of abject poverty of the teeming millions in the midst of the ill-gotten, inflated wealth of a few millionaires caused the reaction against capitalism to burst in all its fury. Defence based on ideology began tottering and political exigencies compelled some concern for improving the lot of the common man. When it came to finding an answer to the concrete problems of economic justice, the modernists made attempts at tailoring Islam according to the Western notions of economic development. And, to our dismay, some of the politically-minded *'ulamā'* found it easy to copy out for Islam that brand of patched capitalism which some Western countries, particularly Britain, have evolved to meet socialism half-way in a realistic effort to stave off the evil day.

The present book is mainly concerned with the concrete economic system of Islam. The religious faith (disparaged by the popular designation "ideology") is referred to only in so far as it motivates and characterises the system. In dealing with the concrete problems of economic life, controversies around the accepted principles of Islam such as the prohibition of *ribā* are discarded. Attention is focussed on agricultural land tenure and the methods of industrialism, which violate the fundamental guarantees of Islam in regard to the free character of the gifts of Nature, the freedom of trade, the operation of the natural factors of supply and demand and the maintenance of the gold standard. The problems arising out of the above violations are not cured by the prohibition of *ribā*, which is often regarded as the panacea for all ills. Even if the banks substitute partnership in business for interest on deposits, the evil consequences of a middleman intervening between the investor and the manager cannot be easily overlooked. Priorities of planning by the State are all-important for economic justice and social welfare. My efforts shall be amply repaid if only the attention of the readers is directed to the problems casually dismissed or scantily treated so far.

I owe a debt of gratitude to my revered teacher, Dr Abid Ahmedali, for his kind encouragement, suggestions and deep interest in the preparation of the book.

S. M. YUSUF

CONTENTS

Chapters

COLLECTIVE SOCIAL SECURITY

The Prophet: "Whatsoever the people of a locality in whose midst a single person remains afflicted with hunger, they are sure to fall from the Grace of Allah" (*Musnad 'Aḥmad*)

Chapter I

THE GENERAL OUTLOOK ON ECONOMICS

(1) Matā'—*Exploitation of Natural Resources*

The economic activity begins when man applies his intelligence and labour to the exploitation and utilisation of the resources of Nature. He is impelled to such activity by the physical need for the sustenance of life. He is spurred on to pursue this activity further and further by his innate desire for more and more amenities and comforts, aided by his unlimited capacity for imagination, refinement of taste and aesthetic enjoyment.

Man's intelligence-labour can produce nothing by itself, being only one of the two primary factors of production. The other factor, of equal importance, is the material resources of Nature, to the exploitation and utilisation of which the intelligence-labour of man is applied.

In the Qur'ān the exploitation and utilisation of the material resources of Nature is termed *Matā'* (متاع) :

On earth will be your dwelling-place and your means of livelihood (*matā'*) for a time (ii. 36).

By His own design Allah "has subjected to you [mankind], as from Him, all that is in the heavens and on earth" (Qur., xlv. 13). The vast resources of Nature are there as a reality which cannot fail to invite the attention and excite the curiosity of man. The responses of Nature are assured by universal, immutable laws. Man has the natural urge and the physical necessity to tap the resources and evoke the productive responses of Nature by the development of his knowledge and skill and the investment of his labour. The resultant economic activity fructifying in man's enjoyment of sustenance, prosperity and power is in full accord with the purpose and scheme of creation and has full approval and encouragement of the Creator :

It is He Who hath created for you all things that are on earth (Qur., ii. 29).

It is We Who have placed you with authority on earth, and provided you therein with means for the fulfilment of your life (vii. 10).

It is Allah Who has subjected the sea to you, that ships may sail through it by His command, that you may seek of His Bounty, and that you may be grateful (xlv. 12).

And We sent down Iron; in which is (material for) mighty war, as well as many benefits for mankind (lvii. 25).

From the religious point of view, the emphasis is on the resources of Nature as a bounty of the Creator. From the economic viewpoint also it is to be underscored that the resources of Nature constitute a primary factor in economic activity and production of all kind.

It follows that Allah gifted man with intelligence-labour, laid bare before him the vast resources of Nature and approved and encouraged the fullest exploitation and utilisation of them by man for his needs and comforts.

(2) *Science and Religion*

So far as the development of intelligence-labour is concerned, religion has no business to fetter the freedom of man to pursue his way through experimentation, trial and error and scientific study and research. The tendency to turn to religion and revelation for guidance in scientific matters was discountenanced when the Prophet declared: "You know best the matters concerning this world of yours." It so happened that the Prophet failed to see any point in fecundation, i.e. grafting part of the male upon the female date-palm tree. So the people of Medina gave up the practice. As the yield declined because of non-fertilisation, the Prophet deposed that it was a matter of human experience rather than Divine revelation. "I am but a human being. When I command you in regard to something of your religion, adhere strictly to it. But when I direct you about something in exercise of my own opinion, then I am just a human being," he explained.[1] Further, the Prophet directed two of his companions to go to Jurash al-Yaman to learn the manufacture of arms there.[2] If it had anything to do with revelation the Prophet would not have turned to the specialist in the field.

Science is discovered, technical skill is acquired, and not revealed. To turn to revelation in this regard is only symptomatic of shameful failure in self-realisation on the part of man. It betrays a false notion of religion and a denial of the wisdom of Divine dispensation.

In regard to the resources of Nature Islam has only warned man that certain items are devoid of utility value, being harmful to his physical and moral welfare. This is just like the manufacturer's warning superinscribed on the labels of dangerous medicines. Such items are like wine, pork and carcass. These particular items are divested of economic value for the Muslims. The non-Muslims remain free to look upon, and deal in, them like any other commodity. With these few exceptions, the vast inexhaustible resources of the entire world are offered FREE as a gift from the Creator to mankind as a whole. The conception of a free

1. Muslim, *Ṣaḥiḥ*, chap. "al-Faḍā'il".
2. Ṭabarī, year 8 H.; 'Ibn Hishām (Ghazwat al-Ṭā'if).

gift of the resources of Nature from the Creator to the Best of Creation is basic to the economic system of Islam. In view of its far-reaching moral import we may as well call it the corner-stone of economic justice.

On the exploitation and utilisation of the resources of Nature Islam sets no limits. At the same time the development of economy, the sophistication of the means of production, the growth of quantity and improvement of quality of all kinds of products are recognised to belong to the domain of science and technology and not of religion. Hence Islam only gives the green signal to, and wholeheartedly welcomes, all advancement in science and technology, which, however, is left to the initiative and enterprise of man.

(3) *Economic System and the Means of Production*

What Islam is concerned with is the establishment of an economic system which is viable enough to ensure, under all the progressive stages of economic development, two broad objectives, viz. (*a*) the satisfaction of the basic needs of life for all the members of the society including those who may be incapacitated or handicapped in one way or the other and (*b*) a just reward of extra comfort and elegance to the talented members for their superior skill and enterprise through lawful means.

It is often contended these days that the socio-economic system is essentially a reflex of the means of production in vogue at a particular stage of economic development in a particular society. The contention is highly misleading; it is wrong in conception and false on factual grounds. The improvement and sophistication of the means of production is an achievement of science and technology, which is cumulative and universal. With necessary talent, urge and determination, facilities and organisation, science and technology would flourish and show similar results in improving the means of production anywhere in the world irrespective of the prevalent economic system. In contrast with it, the economic system is the embodiment of the notions of economic and social justice held by a people. The economic system is concerned with the acquisition, ownership and distribution of wealth and the ways of dealing with it for the satisfaction of one's needs and desires and the promotion of the economy and social welfare of the community. The technology of production is essentially the same in the capitalist and communist countries. The achievement of Marx, Lenin and Mao-tse-Tung is the revolutionary change in the economic system of Russia and China and not the science and technology which they took over from the advanced countries of their time. Japan also took over science and technology from the West but would not revolutionise her economic system on the pattern of her neighbours. In Russia the economic system did not change because of a revolution in the means of production; rather the means of production improved in the wake of the revolution. To take an example, improvement in the ways and means of medical treatment is the sphere of science; provision of medical facilities to the people is part of the economic system. The recent blending in modern China of Western medicine with the indigenous system is pure science and no communism. Even a diehard anti-communist would fain avail himself of it. If the economic system were essentially bound up with the technology of production, then no economic system could claim to be final or durable for long because of the unlimited possibilities of rapid advances in science and technology. Of course, possession and ownership of the means of production is an important subject to be dealt with in an economic system, but the technology of production stands quite apart from it. It is also true that the outlook on material wealth is an important determinant of the pattern of social relationship in a community. Anyway, there is nothing strange or untenable in the claim for an economic system to be viable through all the progressive stages of development in science and technology and improvement and sophistication of the means of production.

(4) *The Basic Needs and Extra Comforts*

The basic needs are food, clothing and shelter.[3] Every individual member of the society is entitled to the full satisfaction of these needs.

The standard of satisfaction of these basic needs is determined by the level of technical know-how and production of goods and services in a particular society. For example, in a developed society water on tap and electricity and gas and, in a highly developed society, a refrigerator and a heater may become part of the basic necessity of housing. Of course, the history of the Islamic civilisation shows that top priority was given to medical attendance and education as soon as the resources of the community—public as well as private—expanded to allow of the same. In short, the satisfaction of the basic needs is not static at low level; it rises with the development of economy until the extra comforts and amenities of today become the necessities of tomorrow. The stable pyramidical society is set for progressive economic development in such a way that the base is broadened

3. The three basic needs are sufficiently indicated in the following verses of the Qur'ān:

But he (father) shall bear the cost of their (mothers') food and clothing on equitable terms (ii. 233).

Let the women live (in *'iddat*) in the same style as ye live (lxv. 6).

'Ibn Ḥazm (*al-Muḥallā*, VI, 156, No. 725) is quite explicit about it:

"يلزم ان يقام للفقراء بما يأكلون من القوت الذى لا بد منه ، و باللباس للشتاء والصيف بمثل ذلك ، و بمسكن يكنهم من المطر و الصيف و الشمس و عيون المارة" ـ

in proportion to the rise of the apex.

Upon the broad base of the provision of the necessities of life for each and every member of the society the specially talented ones are offered full opportunity and incentive to build the superstructure of extra comforts and amenities for the few as a just reward for intelligence-labour with proper safeguards against the exploitation of the less gifted masses. Abstinence from pleasure as such, self-privation and lack of interest in better comfort and elegance is against human nature and no virtue at all. "Monkery has not been prescribed for us," said the Prophet.[4] Allah did not ordain it for the followers of Jesus also ; they just invented it.[5]

As against it, there is every encouragement to better living :

Say : Who hath forbidden the beautiful (gifts) of Allah, which He hath provided for His servants, and the things clean and pure (which He hath provided) for sustenance (Qur., vii. 32).

O ye who believe ! eat of the good things that We have provided for you, and be grateful to God, if it is Him ye worship (ii. 172).

O ye who believe ! make not unlawful the good things which Allah hath made lawful for you, but commit no excess : for Allah loveth not those given to excess. Eat of the things which Allah hath provided for you, lawful and good, but fear Allah, in Whom ye believe (v. 90-91).

(5) *The Basic Economic Problem*

In an organised society the basic economic problem is not the increase in production or the rise in National Income, but the enforcement of a system, supported by the collective moral conscience of the society and the legal authority of the State, which

4. Aḥmad b. Ḥanbal, *Musnad* (al-Maimaniyyah, 1313 H.), VI, 226.

5. "But the monasticism which they invented for themselves, We did not prescribe for them : (We commanded) only the seeking for the Good Pleasure of Allah ; but that they did not foster as they should have done" (lvii. 27).

is designed to ensure the satisfaction of the basic needs (as mentioned above) to each and every individual member of the society. The fate of the less gifted toiling masses cannot be left to the oppressive forces operative in the so-called Free Economy. The State has to see and to intervene, in so far as it is necessary, to provide opportunities for work to every member according to his capacity and to ensure the satisfaction of the basic needs of life for each and every member of the society. This is the primary responsibility of the State. In our own time the developing countries became preoccupied with industrialisation and planning for increased production to the utter neglect of this primary responsibility of the State, which called for a radical change in the economic system. The national income of the oil-rich Emirates has risen to fabulous figures but the basic needs of the masses remain unsatisfied because of the continuance of an unjust economic system. Hence the economic ills and the social and political unrest in the developing countries.

It is curious indeed that when the developing countries started on the road to industrialism, there were few who realised that capitalism was coming into the bargain. Quite complacently it was assumed that only science and technology were being taken over from the West. No thought was given to the admissibility of the means and methods of industrialism from the viewpoint of economic and social justice. Foreign aid was eagerly sought for unmindful of its effects on the economic and political freedom. Today we have naked capitalism before us. Its horrors have caused the ideological conflict to burst in all its fury.

(6) *The Fundamentals of Islamic Economic System*

The economic system of Islam is based on the fundamental assumption that if a man is given the opportunity of applying his intelligence-labour to the wherewithal of economic activity, viz. a share in the material resources as a free gift of Nature, he will always be able to produce, at the minimum, enough to satisfy his basic needs of life. If a man is capable of work, possessing a sound mind in a sound body, but would not engage himself in productive activity, the society and the State shall refuse to support him until he is compelled to work for himself. If a man is incapable of work, the society and the State shall help and support him through appropriate provisions in the economic system. If a man is both capable and willing to work, yet unable to find the means and the opportunity for it, it will be the responsibility of the State to provide him with the means and the opportunity for work, and with honourable sustenance and support until the man is able to support himself.

In this connection it is of vital importance that the economic system should guarantee through statutory provisions an *equitable* distribution of the free gifts of Nature among the members of the society. At the root of all economic disequilibrium, causing unemployment and unequal opportunities and unjust reward for skill and labour, is the maldistribution of the free gifts of Nature at the primary stage of economic development. When an undue advantage accrues to a class of people in the possession and ownership of the gifts of Nature beyond their legitimate and equitable share in them, it reduces the rest of the people to destitution and helplessness, thus opening the door wide open for exploitation in the form of rent for the free gifts of Nature and unfair wages.

It must be added here that it is not the duty of the State, rather it is illegitimate and unlawful on the part of a State, to tax directly or indirectly the general body of consumers and to give "protection" to the interests of a class of producers in the name of industrialisation. Commercial and industrial enterprise

belongs to the private sector ; it has a natural and really beneficial growth in the open space of free competition and not in the hot-house of tariff barriers, foreign exchange restrictions and internal price control. Thus it will be seen that the modern developing States have not only neglected their primary duty of ensuring the satisfaction of the basic needs of each and every individual ; on the contrary, they have occupied themselves with industrialisation through means which have only made the rich richer and the poor poorer. The growth in the G.N.P. only swells the bellies of a few, while the common people are called upon to tighten the belt under compulsion of the authority of the State.

(7) *Function of the State in Economic Development*

If every capable member had the will to work and the opportunity to do so with his equitable share of the FREE gifts of Nature, there would always be enough to satisfy the basic needs of all, no matter whether the society were developed or undeveloped. The progress of science and technology should contribute to the satisfaction of the basic needs for every individual member of the society at a higher level. On the contrary, if improved methods of production result in the concentration of wealth in a few hands and abject poverty and ruthless exploitation of the toiling masses, obviously the economic system is at fault. The remedy lies not in increasing the overall production but in reforming and changing the economic system.

This is not to say that economic development should stop at a particular point or a particular time. Given the opportunity and the incentive, the talented and the enterprising members of the society shall always be accelerating economic development at a steady pace and building up the apex of extra comforts and amenities for the few. But that is essentially the function of the gifted members acting privately and individually or in co-operation with each other. The State can only help in raising the level of technical know-how through educative methods with equal opportunities for all. But the primary objective of the economic system and the special function of the State is to ensure that the gifted members get the just reward, no more and no less, for their skill and enterprise, and that the less gifted members are in the process subjected to no exploitation of their money and labour. Taxing the general body of consumers, either directly or indirectly, and employing methods of "protection" to promote economic enterprise by a few is only tantamount to the State acting as a cat's-paw for the vested interests. In the very nature of things the prosperity resulting from State support and protection to the gifted members of the society is prosperity for the few resting on the poverty and the misery of the many.

(8) *Industrialism* vis-a-vis *Nationalism*

It is curious indeed that industrialism as a prime policy of the State propelled by the force of nationalism should become the order of the day. Toynbee has quite poignantly traced the ills of the present-day world to the contradiction between industrialism and nationalism. In his own words :

> The general state of economic equilibrium at low tension on a minute scale was violently disturbed by the advent of Industrialism ; for Industrialism, like Democracy, is intrinsically cosmopolitan in its operations. If the real essence of Democracy is, as the French Revolution delusively proclaimed, a spirit of fraternity, the essential requirement of Industrialism, if it is to achieve its full potentiality, is world-wide co-operation. . . . Finding the world divided into small economic units, Industrialism set to work, a hundred and fifty years ago, to re-shape the economic structure of the world in two ways, both leading in the direction

of world unity. It sought to make the economic units fewer and bigger, and also to lower the barriers between them.

It we glance at the history of these efforts we shall find that there was a turning-point in it round about the sixties and seventies of the last century. Down to that date Industrialism was assisted by Democracy in its efforts to diminish the number of economic units and to lower the barriers between them. After that date both Industrialism and Democracy reversed their policies and worked in the opposite direction.[6]

It is this democracy plus industrialism *in collision with* nationalism which is the ruling passion of the newly independent developing nations of the East, who despise and imitate the West at one and the same time.[7]

(9) *Questionable Methods of Industrialism*

As pointed out above, industrialism is achieved mainly through taxation, tightening the belt of the common people, foreign aid (in most cases a halter round the neck), and, above all, protective measures, i.e. tariff and trade barriers, exchange restrictions and monetary controls. All these measures are the very negation of the cosmopolitan spirit. It is amazing that the validity of taxation and protection for industrialism is seldom examined, far less questioned. Why should the common people be taxed to prop up industries owned by a few millionaires? Why should the common people be compelled to pay an in-competitive higher price for low quality products just to maintain enterprises in which they have no stake and no interest at all? Why should the industrial magnates appropriate to themselves the profits made up of forcible extortions from the cornered helpless consumers? Why should the common people suffer for a life-

6. A. Toynbee, *A Study of History*, p. 728

7. See also my *Some Aspects of Islamic Culture* (Lahore : 1961, Institute of Islamic Culture), p. 34.

time from the evils of an artificially controlled economy such as shortage of essential commodities, adulteration and blackmarketing—for the sake of industrialism ? Obviously, the common people bear all the burdens of industrialism. What do they actually get in return for the same ?—A rise in G.N.P. and in average national income ! ! ! Highly deceptive terms designed to cover up the growing inequity in the distribution of growing national wealth.

When the strain reaches the breaking point, palliatives of socialistic measures are resorted to such as nationalisation, fixation of minimum wages and allocation of shares to the workers in the capital and the profits of the enterprises served by them. Similarly, price controls and marketing regulations are enforced to keep within bearable limits the rigours of industrialism as a policy of the State. Islam substitutes *equitable* distribution of national wealth for industrialism as the prime policy of the State. It questions the validity of taxation and protection for industrialism from the viewpoint of economic justice and morality. Once protective measures are ruled out, the need for nationalisation and price control does not arise at all.

(10) *No Bias against Non-Muslims in Economic Activities*

Islam adheres strictly to the unequivocal and irrevocable stand that the progress of science and technology and the consequent development of economy is free, objective, experimental, cumulative and universal. No difference of religious faith or of nationality is allowed to hamper the economic activity of man on the widest scale or to deny or grudge the just reward for skill and labour to a fellow human being.

Allah is not the God of the Muslims alone. He is the sustainer of the entire universe (*Rabb-ul-'Ālamīn*) in which both the

Muslims and the non-Muslims have an equal span of life. It is not only a good pious belief; it has active cultural implications too. It is this belief which inoculates a Muslim against any jealousy of the economic prosperity of his non-Muslim neighbour. Islam never holds before its followers the bait of pestilence, poverty and hunger for the non-Muslims. Allah would not exercise His authority over the earth to prevent it from yielding to a non-Muslim agriculturist the fruits of his labour. Similarly, if a non-Muslim business man thrives in the midst of the Muslims, it is just his due. Hence Islam allows the fullest scope of partnership between Muslims and non-Muslims in the economic field; excepting a few stipulations in regard to the commodities prohibited for the Muslims, there are practically no restrictions on commercial exchange either within the lands of Islam or outside. That is why it never occurred to any Muslim government to squeeze out the non-Muslims from any particular field of economic activity through a calculated plan and deliberate policy. Rather all the evidence points to the contrary.[8]

(11) *Economic Justice, A Moral Virtue*

The concern for the satisfaction of the basic needs of every individual member of the society and for maintaining the standards of justice and equity in the development of economy in all the aspects alluded to above is grounded in the moral conscience of man.

Laws are, no doubt, indispensable for the maintenance of peace and justice in an organised society, but respect for, and compliance with, the law is primarily a matter of psychology. The same is the case with democracy, which is more a matter of spirit than that of an external framework. In the words of

8. Ibid., pp. 35-6.

Toynbee : "Love of mankind has been a force in history but only when it is a by-product of an intense love of God Exploitation does breed hatred, but if the campaign against exploitation were based on moral grounds, it would be unnecessary to exploit class-hatred for its success.

Early socialistic movements in the first half of the nineteenth century originated in the moral conscience of virtuous men who, in most cases, were infused with a religious spirit. A religion which deadens the sense of equity and justice is certainly an opiate. But it would be a folly to discard a religion which provides the motive force behind equity in the framework of economic activity and equality in social relationship. Iqbal pleaded for the same when he said :

Modern atheistic socialism, which possesses all the fervour of a new religion, has a broader outlook ; but having received its philosophical basis from the Hegelians of the left wing, it rises in revolt against the very source which could have given it strength and purpose. Both nationalism and atheistic socialism, at least in the present state of human adjustments, must draw upon the psychological forces of hate, suspicion, and resentment which tend to impoverish the soul of man and close up his hidden sources of spiritual energy.[9]

9. ***Reconstruction of Religious Thought in Islam***, Lecture VII: "Is Religion Possible ? " (Lahore : 1962, Sh. Muhammad Ashraf), p. 188.

Chapter II

THE ACQUISITION OF WEALTH

(1) *Economic Activity : A Moral Obligation*

The need to exert one's self and work for producing, earning and bringing about the satisfaction of one's desires is quite natural. But of all the creatures man is distinguished by *will*, which can either strengthen and accelerate or resist and retard the course of Nature. Hence Islam recognises the physical and the economic factors but does not leave man's behaviour and activity to those factors alone. Rather it concerns itself mainly with reinforcing the will by inducing the appropriate psychological and moral state of mind and conscience. In this way man becomes an active participant in the processes of Nature and of history, and gets the credit for volition in addition to the material benefits which accrue from science and economics. In Islam economic activity is stressed as a moral obligation. Material benefits flow from morality in action. Honesty is a moral value before experience proves it to be the best policy.

Exertion in economic production as a moral obligation is stressed frequently in the Qur'ān :

It is He Who has made the earth manageable for you, so traverse ye through its tracts and enjoy of the sustenance which He furnishes (lxvii. 15).

Generally the economic activity is termed "seeking the bounty of Allah" (ابتغاء فضل الله). The Prophet's Traditions provide due amplification and illustration with concrete examples of the injunction above : The Prophet kissed the hands of Sa'd b. Mu'ādh which were hardened with manual labour, and declared : These are the very palms that are loved by Allah.[1] He also stressed that "None of you ever took food better than that earned with one's own hand."[2] 'Umar understood best and enforced relentlessly the true spirit of Islam. He passed by a group of Qur'ān-readers who were sitting with their heads bent down. He was told that they were *mutawakkilūn* (resigned to fate). Thereupon he exclaimed : No. Rather they are *muta'akkilūn*, i.e. parasites who consumed other people's money. The true *mutawakkil* is one who sows the seed and depends on Allah for its germination.[3] He is also reported to have said : On being impressed by a man I ask if he practises some craft. If the answer were in the negative, the man falls low in my estimation.[4]

(2) *Ownership in Islam*

The essence of the economic activity of man is the exploitation and utilisation of the productive forces of Nature with his

1. *Usd-ul-Ghābah*, on Sa'd :

ان رسول الله (صلعم) صافح سعد بن معاذ (رض) فاذا يداه قدا كتبتا ، فسأله النبى (صلعم) عن ذلک فقال : أضرب بالمر و المسحاة لأنفق على عيالى، فقبل رسول الله (صلعم) يده و قال : كفان يحبهما الله تعالى ۔

2. Al-Bukhārī, *Ṣaḥīḥ* (Delhi : 1354 H., Mujtabā'ī Press), I, 278 :

"ما أكل أحد طعاما قط خيرا من عمل يده" ۔

3 - روى ان عمر مر بقوم من القراء فرآهم جلوسا قد نكسوا رؤوسهم فقال : من هولاء ؟ فقيل: هم المتوكلون ، فقال : كلا ، هم المتأكلون يأكلون أموال الناس، ألا أنبئكم من المتوكلون ؟ فقيل : نعم ، فقال هوالذى يلقى الحب فى الأرض ثم يتوكل على ربه عزوجل ۔

The shrewd and sarcastic distinction between المتوكل and المتأكل is a treat for the students of religion as well as literature.

4 - "انى لأرى الرجل فيعجبنى ، فأقول : أله حرفة ؟ فان قالوا : لا ، سقط فى عينى" ۔

intelligence-labour. It follows that man needs primarily a share in the material resources as a free gift of Nature to take off on the course of economic development. Human nature demands, and reason permits, that every individual should appropriate to himself such share of the original wherewithal of economic activity as he can, according to his capacity, manage and actually put to use with his intelligence-labour. This process of appropriating certain material resources for the application of one's intelligence-labour and obtaining "desirabilities" (satisfactions/utilities) therefrom is covered by the institution of ownership.

The exact connotation of ownership in Islam has to be made clear and distinguished from usages in other economic systems. Allah is the Creator-Owner and Lord Sovereign of "all that is in the heavens and in the earth". He is also the "Lord Sustainer of all the worlds". Everything belongs to Him. Only He has delegated to man the authority and the power to exploit and utilise the resources of Nature "for a time". This delegation of authority and power is called *'istikhlāf* (استخلاف)—literally, appointing a Khalīfah or an agent—and *imdād* (امداد), i.e. aid for economic activity.[5] Thus, in precise terms, man is only a delegatee who utilises what is actually owned by Allah. Where the Omnipotence of Allah is emphasised, the riches of the world are ascribed to Him :

Give them something yourselves out of the means which Allah has given to you (xxiv. 33).

And where the actual use of the riches is kept in view man is called the possessor of wealth :

Of their goods take alms (ix. 103).

The wealth that ye have gained (ix. 24).

Nor will his wealth profit him when he falls headlong (into

5. *Vide* Qur'ān, lvii. 7 and lxxi. 12.

the Fire) (xcii. 11).

It has further to be noted that Allah delegated the authority in respect of the utilisation of material aid for economic activity to the entire mankind as a whole over the entire riches of the world taken together. As pointed out above, there is no distinction between a Muslim and a Kāfir in the matter. This is not merely a religious belief or an abstract metaphysical idea. As a matter of fact, it embodies and invests with religious sanctity the basic principles underlying the various institutions of ownership —private and otherwise—sanctioned by Islam. In actual practice the aforesaid principle has the following ramifications :

(*a*) That ownership signifies essentially the right to exploit and utilise the wealth. This right is, of course, transferable through the recognised method.

(*b*) That the owner deserves the ownership only so long as he exploits and utilises the wealth.

(*c*) That the owner who ceases to exploit and utilise his wealth is induced and even forced by various means to part with his idle possessions.

(*d*) That in no case is an owner allowed to charge rent for a free gift of Nature from a fellow human being, who has an equal claim to a share in the wherewithal of economic activity.

Clearly the target is to keep economic activity at the optimum through one agency or the other.

(3) *Private Ownership*

An individual exercises the authority delegated to mankind in general by appropriating for himself a share in the total resources of the world offered as a free gift of Nature. This is called private ownership and it does not apply to all the natural resources indiscriminately. It is confined to such natural resources as depend for their cultivation and growth on human skill and labour. It extends to all such items of moveable and immoveable property as lend themselves for possession and utilisation by an individual without in any way contravening the individual or collective rights and interests of others. Private property, in so far as it is premissible, is sacred and inviolable on a par with the life of the owner.[6] It is important to note that the legitimate and lawful gains in money and property are assured protection, not only from the depradations of the anti-social elements, but also from the unauthorised and wilful extortions of the government.

From the Islamic point of view, the abolition of private property or its quantitative limitation by fixed ceilings is against human nature. Both the ways curb initiative and enterprise, smother real talent and turn the producers of wealth into slaves of these who somehow set themselves up to run the government and control the economy. On the other hand, if the institution of private property were not regulated by considerations of economic justice, it would soon result in the concentration of wealth in fewer and fewer hands and callous exploitation of the rest. Islam, therefore, regulates the process, and specifies and defines the means, of acquisition in such a way as to eliminate exploitation and *chance*. For example, *ribā* and all forms of gambling are declared unlawful. In a nutshell, Islam ensures that wealth is always a fair return for labour.

(4) *Ownership of Land*

The conditions of ownership in Islam work out to ensure that where labour is invested in the free gifts of Nature the value of the product involves no rent for the gifts which are initially free

6. In this respect أموال and دماء are often coupled together as, for example, in the Farewell Address of the Prophet on the Mount 'Arafāt.

and should throughout remain free. This is poignantly illustrated by the stipulations of Islam in règard to land:

(*a*) *'Iḥyā' al-Mawāt* (احياءالموات). Whoever puts to proper use a piece of virgin land, he becomes the owner of it.[7] The proper use means agriculture, horticulture (or, for the matter of that, a similar use for productive purposes) and housing. Virgin land is defined as that which no one has yet laid a claim to for utilisation. And the ownership is hedged round with the important condition of actual utilisation. This is the way of an individual claiming and reserving for himself a reasonable share in the endowments of Nature, which are free for mankind as a whole. The Prophet has also specified a limit of three years for bringing into actual use the plot taken possession of by an individual. If he fails to do so, the land will revert to the State.[8]

(*b*) *Al-'Iqṭā'* (الاقطاع). The function of the State is to husband the economy and promote the optimum use of land for production. In pursuit of the same it has the right to allocate to active and capable tenants such land as is lying virgin or has fallen into disuse and reverted to it. Of course, the State is prohibited from charging any price or fee (apart from development charges) for the free endowment of Nature. The allocation is to be made on the usual condition of payment of *kharāj*/*'ushr*. It will be seen that this right of the State does not open a loophole for the growth of the *jāgīrdārī* or the feudal system associated with an

7. 'Abū Dāwūd, *Sunan*, No. 3076 :

عن عروة قال : أشهد ان رسول الله قضى ان الأرض أرض الله ، والعباد عباد الله ، و من أحيا مواتا فهوأ حق به'' ـ

8. 'Abū Yūsuf, *Kitāb al-Kharāj* (al-Maṭba'at al-Salafīyah), p 65 :

''عادى الأرض لله و لرسوله ثم لكم من بعد ، فمن أحيا أرضاً ميتة فهى له ، و ليس لمحتجر حق بعد ثلاث سنوات'' ـ

unjust and undemocratic society. *'Iqṭā'* as a term of Islamic *Fiqh* has nothing to do with *'Iqṭā'* as a careless and misleading translation of feudalism.

(*c*) Taking into account the wide variation in the aptitude and the capacity of individuals for management and labour, the size of land-holding is limited not by a uniform arbitrary ceiling but by the extent of actual cultivation on the part of the tenant by himself and with the help of hired labour. Apart from labour the cultivator is to employ his own tools, equipment, animals, seed, etc. If a capable and willing cultivator is destitute of initial resources, it is the duty af the State to help him with gifts of money or interest-free loans. Otherwise the cultivator can take the implements on simple hire without sharing with the owner of the implements the produce of agriculture, which is the result of his own labour. Thus the Islamic system ensures free play of the initiative and intelligence-labour of an individual while guarding against exploitation of the less gifted members and the levy of rent for the endowments of Nature.

(*d*) It must be remembered that the ownership of agricultural land is different from the ownership of moveable property or even non-agricultural land. The retention of the ownership of agricultural land is conditional upon its proper use by the owner himself. If he does not use it properly for there years, he is compelled to part with it in favour of someone else. Further, the owner has no right to let out agricultural land on rent, be it in cash or in crop. The net result is that the agricultural land retains throughout its character of a free gift of Nature, which is claimed by an individual for actual use only. Under no circumstances is an individual entitled to charge rent for an endowment of Nature from a fellow human being, who in his own right is a cosharer in the endowment.

(5) *Metayer-Tenure and Lease of Agricultural Land*[9]

In Islam the right of ownership of agricultural land is, of course, unquestionable. This, however, does not presuppose the unrestricted right to let out such land on rent just as the right to own money does not imply the right to practise usury. Agriculture involves, on the one hand, "the original and indestructible powers of land," which is a gift of Nature, and, on the other hand, the initial cost of developing virgin land, the wherewithal of farming, i.e. the seed, manure and implements, and the farmer's labour in tending a crop—all of which come under investment and labour. If one analyses the traditions of Islam, one finds a clear distinction made between the gifts of Nature (*natural capital*) and the labour of man. The Prophet underlined this distinction by enjoining upon his followers to respect the basic rights of others in what "they did not produce with their own hands."[10] Gifts of Nature are free for the use of all; one has a right only to such share of them as one can actually consume or put to profitable use without detriment to the legitimate share of others. This principle is fully recognised in regard to water, salt, forests, pastures and the like. Any undue extension of the rights of one member of the society as against the rest is *ḥimā* if it be through force, and tantamount to *ḥimā*, to monopoly and corner-market if it be through attachment by sale—all of which practices are condemned as anti-social and banned in no uncertain terms. It is in conformity with this general principle that virgin land is free and belongs to the one who cares to develop it. It is the labour and the expenditure involved in bringing the

9. For a detailed discussion on the subject, see my *Studies in Islamic History and Culture* (Lahore : 1970, Institute of Islamic Culture), Chap. VII.

10. *Vide Mishkāt* (Delhi : 1307 H. Mujtabā'ī Press), p. 259 : "ماء لم تعمل يداك," i.e. water, which you have not made with your own hands.

land under the plough—no matter whether incurred by State or by an individual—which sets a price on land and determines its ownership. But once this process of buying and selling starts a stage is soon reached when a person owns more than what he can himself manage. The position of such a person is not different from that of a capitalist seeking the partnership of labour for the exploitation of his savings. It is inconceivable that Islam should enact stringent restrictions upon partnership between capital and labour in the field of commerce and neglect to regulate the same kind of partnership in agriculture. The society of the 'Anṣār in Medina was agricultural if the milieu at Mecca was commercial and the evils of exploitation were as manifest in the one as in the other. Actually we find that by and large the same prohibitions apply to both. We notice first that *al-mukhāṭarah* (the advantage of a mere chance) is to be guarded against in agriculture as scrupulously as in commerce. Hence, the ban on the practice most common in the days of *al-Jāhiliyyah*, according to which land was let out with the stipulation that the produce of a particular part of it (usually with greater prospects of fertility) should go to the owner. Similarly, the practice of letting out the land on a fixed amount of produce was also declared unlawful as it stood obviously on a par with interest in business and commerce. There only remained a third practice of letting out the land on payment of a stipulated proportion of the actual produce. This practice, it is on record, was brought to the notice of the Prophet, who only replied : "An owner should cultivate the land himself, else bestow it on his brother ; failing both it was up to him to cling to the land (without putting it to any use)."[11]

11 - من كانت له أرض فليزرعها ، أوليمنحها أخاه ، فان ابى فليمسك أرضه -

It remains a fact that this practice, which may be called *al-muzāra'ah* proper, became widespread among the *Ṣaḥābah*. But at the same time there is ample evidence, direct as well as indirect, to show that grave doubts about it were entertained long after the death of the Prophet. Significant is also the suggestion of al-Ḥasan al-Baṣrī, probably derived from the practice of 'Umar, that the owner of land should also take a share in investment and/or labour with the other party so that his share in the produce may not constitute a return for the gifts of Nature only.[12] Of the great jurists 'Abū Ḥanīfah ruled out *al-muzāra'ah* as unlawful. Al-Shāfi'ī approved of it only on the analogy of *al-musāqāt* in the particular cases of vines and dates. But the Prophet's dealing with the Jews of Khaibar and the arrangement approved by him as between the 'Anṣār and the Muhājirīn, on which the analogy was ba ed, could not really be called *al-musāqāt*. Later jurists, disposed as they were to bow to the actual practice (*al-ta'āmul*), made a meagre attempt to draw a parallel between *al-muzāra'ah* and *al-mudā.abah*. They, however, disregarded the vital fact, of which they do show a cognizance here and there, that *al-muzāra'ah* involved the forces of Nature, whereas *al-muḍārabah* did not. A return on investment and labour is perfectly justified but exploitation starts when one person arrogates to himself the right to charge another one a price for any gift of Nature. Rent as defined by Ricardo is a clear case of unearned income with all the evils, moral and social, attendant upon it. And it is amply recognised by all, the *fuqahā'* as well as the modern economists, that it is impossible to separate the contribution of investment and labour from that of Nature to the produce of agriculture. Thus it will be seen that metayer-tenure runs counter to the general principles of Islam and, on the

12. Al-Bukhāri, op. cit., I, 313.

admission of the great jurists themselves, is allowed merely on the ground of *al-ta'āmul.*

But if this were so, what about the practice of letting out agricultural land on a fixed sum of money? The practice was not in vogue in the days of the Prophet. Curiously enough, it grew as a way of escaping the grave doubts in regard to the admissibility of metayer-tenure. Legists like 'Ibn 'Abbās thought of relieving the conscience of the people by giving the relationship between the land-owner and the tenant the form of *al-'ijārah,* i.e. lease. But whatever the form and name given to it the crux of the matter is to inquire into the sanction behind this kind of relationship. Was it approved by the Prophet? No. Was it envisaged by him either as *al-muzāra'ah* or as *al-'ijārah*? No. On the contrary, all that the Prophet is reported to have said, either under the heading of *al-muzāra'ah* or *al-'ijārah,* is that a land-owner should cultivate the land himself, else bestow it on his brother; failing both it was up to him to cling to it without any benefit to himself or to others. This last provision is meant only as a reproach and the only alternative left to the land-owner bars his sharing the fruits of the labour of the tenant in any of the two forms, i.e. in the form of a proportionate share of the produce and also in the form of a fixed sum of money. As the people in general lack the generosity to give their land free to others, the injunction of the Prophet was in effect a constraint on the land-owner to part with his surplus land and, of course, a curb on investment in land. It is remarkable that the authenticity of the above saying of the Prophet was never questioned and it was always remembered and quoted on the subject. Nor was its import and implication doubted at any time; only it was interpreted by the legists to indicate a mere preference. Some land-owners like Ṭāwūs b. Kaisān also sought to excuse themselves on the ground of their liberality towards the tenants whom, they asserted, they wanted to help and not to exploit. But still 'Ibn 'Umar would not be satisfied until he gave up renting the land.[13] We also have to recall that the cumulative result of the measures taken by 'Umar I in regard to the administration of the conquered lands was, in the words of Wellhausen, "to divert the acquisitive instinct of the Arabs from land purchases". No wonder that when the system of 'Umar was breached during the reign of his successor, the change proved radical enough to shake the very foundations of the empire.

Though the practice of early Islam is entitled to the highest respect, the persistent doubts concerning the relationship between the landlord and the tenant do warrant a re-examination and fresh understanding of the undoubted injunction or advice of the Prophet on the subject. We can very well appreciate that in the beginning the restriction on investment in land should have proved irksome in the same way as the total ban on interest does to some of our modernists today. But after landlordism has played out the part which at that distant period might have appeared indispensable for development, is it not high time that the wisdom of the Prophet's clear and unambiguous ruling be recognised fully, frankly and rigorously?

(6) *Public Property*

All the resources of Nature which are meant for the common use and convenience of a particular community of people and which, if allowed to pass into private hands, would make it

13. Aḥmad b. Ḥanbal, *Musnad*, II, 6, 64:

" . . . فقال (رافع بن خديج) : نعم ! نهى رسول الله عن كراء المزارع'
فتركها ابن عمر فكان لا يكريها ، فكان اذا سئل يقول : زعم ابن خديج ان
رسول الله نهى عن كراء المزارع" .

difficult for the community to stay together—all such resources are declared to be public propety. The Prophet named three things, viz. water, pasture and fire, not to exhaust the number but to indicate the character thereof.[14] Wild forests, deep seas, lakes and ponds also come within the same category. Wild animals are the free gift of Nature; they become the property of one who exerts himself to capture them (of course, without trespassing the private property of others). All the products of the sea (*saib al-baḥr* =سيب البحر)—fish, amber and pearls—are free for collection and utilisation. 'Umar I is reported to have approved of the levy of one-fifth royalty to the State on amber and the ornamental products of the sea. 'Umar II is said to have reduced the royalty to one-fortieṭh (on the analogy of the *Zakāt*) on large-scale fishing, while 'Alī is credited with the sale of fishing rights in Burs (near Babylon) for 4000 dirhams. But 'Abū Ḥanīfah would stick to the general principle of free use of all the natural sea products. Honey is also free for collection from wild forests. The *'ushr* is to be paid on honey if collected from land which is subject to that levy.[15]

No one is allowed to practise *ḥimā*, i.e. to exercise power to deprive others of their share in the resources of Nature. The State is brought into being just to protect and regulate the natural rights of the people in the natural resources of the country. It cannot change the character of public property in any way. It can only

14. Aḥmad and 'Abū Dāwūd :
"الناس شركاء فى ثلاث : الماء و الكلأ و النار" و فى حديث آخر "والملح" ۔

15. 'Abū Yūsuf, op. cit., pp. 70 and 87 ; 'Abū 'Ubaid, *al-Amwāl*, Nos. 889-90. *Vide* also *al-Muḥallā* (ed. Aḥmad Muḥammad Shākir, 1349 H.), VI, 117 (No. 703) :
"و ليس فى شئ مما أصيب من العنبر و الجواهر و الياقوت والزمرد ۔ بحريه و بريه ۔ شئ أصلا ، و هو كله لمن وجده" ۔

put certain restrictions and make some reservations here and there in the public interest only. For example, the Prophet reserved the land of Naqīʿ for the horses of the cavalry.[16]

The most important item, however, is that of the mineral and other deposits which are in imponderable quantities and inexhaustible. It is reported that the Prophet allotted a piece of land rich in salt deposits at Ma'rib to particular individuals, but as soon as he came to know that the salt there was in the nature of a running stream (الماء العد), i.e. in imponderable quantity and inexhaustible, he hastened to cancel the allotment and declare the deposits to be public property.[17]

If the deposits are in limited quantities they may pass into private ownership which, one is inclined to suppose, was the case with the land allotted by the Prophet to Bilāl b. al-Hārith along

16 - عن ابن عمر ان النبى (صلعم) حمى النقيع للخيل ، خيل المسلمين -

17 - عن ابيض بن حمال انه استقطع رسول الله (صلعم) الملح بمأرب ، فلما ولى قيل يا رسول الله ! أتدرى ما أقطعته له؟ انما أقطعت له المال العد ، قال : فرجعه منه - و فى رواية عن عمرو بن قيس المازنى قال : استقطعت رسول الله (صلعم) معدن الملح بمأرب فأقطعنيه ، فقيل : يا رسول الله ! انه بمنزلة الماء العد - يعنى انه لا ينقطع - فقال رسول الله (صلعم) : فلاً اذن

قال ابو عبيد : وأما اقطاعه (صلعم) أبيض بن حمال المأربى الملح الذى بمأرب ثم ارتجاعه منه ، فانما أقطعه و هو عنده ارض موات يحييها ابيض و يعمرها ، فلما تبين للنبى (صلعم) انه ماء عد - و هو الذى له مادة لاتنقطع مثل ماء العيون والآبار—ارتجعه منه لان سنة رسول الله فى الكلأ والنار و الماء ان الناس جميعا فيه شركاء ، فكره ان يجعله ارجل يحوزه دون الناس— الأموال لأبى عبيد رقم ٦٩٣ ، انظر ايضا الترمذى ، أبواب الأحكام و سنن أبى داؤد رقم ٣٠٦٤ -

with the mountains and the mines thereon.[18] Such limited quantities would not affect the general price level and would not create monopolistic conditions. The State will be entiled to the *khums* (one-fifth royalty). To sum up, all the natural deposits—those which lie on the surface and those which are extracted from underground—are categorised as public property. They include salt, precious stones, gold, silver, iron, lead, coal, beryl and petroleum.

Many legists, particularly Mālik, are opposed to leasing the mines to private concerns. In any case, the State will have to keep a strict watch on the working of the mines to prevent monopolies and undue profits. The ideal way of working the mines on behalf of and for the community as a whole in accordance with the dictates of the Sharī'ah is through State-controlled agencies run on a no-profit basis. This will ensure that the mineral products, when they reach the hands of the consumer, bear a price just equal to the labour involved in extracting the material and refining and getting it ready for use. The price will be free from any rent for the free gift of Nature, and it will not be lawful on the part of the government to impose any kind of tax on the same. Some legists would allow the State to collect at source one-fifth or one-fortieth (*Zakāt*) royalty on extractive industries, particularly in the case of gold and silver.[19]

Highways and roads, dams and canals, public parks and mosques are all, by their very nature, public property. Neither an

18. 'Abū Dāwūd, *Sunan*, Nos. 3062, 3063.

19. 'Abū 'Ubaid, op. cit., Nos. 872 and 873. 'Ibn Ḥazm is quite explicit that the mineral deposits are absolutely free. *Vide al-Muḥallā*, VI, 108 (No. 700):

"لا شئ فى المعادن كلها ، و هى فائدة ، لا خمس و لا زكاة ،عجلة ، فان بقى الذهب و الفضة عند مستخرجها حولا قمريا و كان ذلك مقدار ماتجب فيه الزكاة - زكاه ، و الا فلا " -

individual nor a State has any authority to restrict their use in such a way as to deprive any individual or group of the natural right to the common use of public property.

(7) *State Property*

The State is entrusted with the dispensation of certain moneys and properties in the interests of public welfare. The Khalīfah has the right to exercise his judgment as to how best to deal with them in accordance with the aims and objectives of the Sharī'ah. Excepting the *Zakāt*, whose beneficiaries are specified in the Qur'ān, the management of all the other revenues and properties of the State is left to the discretion of the Chief Executive. The *Kharāj* and the *Jizyah* are the two most important categories of State property in the sense that the State has full authority over their management and dispensation.

All the lands conquered through war or capitulation to a threat of war are treated as *Kharāj* lands. Only the lands of the Arabian Peninsula are an exception to this rule. The ownership of the *Kharāj* lands belongs to the State. The State-ownership of the *Kharāj* lands signifies the common rights of all the Muslims in contemporary and in subsequent times. The individual cultivators are given the title to the use of the lands while the revenue is earmarked for the welfare of the present as well as the future generations of the Muslims.

The *Kharāj* is a fixed sum levied on land, of course, in a reasonable manner so as not to cause any unbearable hardship to the cultivator. It is realised irrespective of whether the land was actually ploughed or not and without reference to the actual yield. The *'ushr.* is one-tenth (in the case of irrigated land one-twentieth) of the actual produce realised in the spirit of a religious obligation and credited to the *Zakāt* fund in the Bait al-Māl.

The revenue of the Bait al-Māl is augmented by income from the properties under the management of the State. There are also two irregular sources of income, namely, *al-fay'* (war booty) and the one-fifth levy on *al-rikāz* (treasure-trove).

(8) *Partnership in Trade and Industry*

There is unlimited scope for expansion in the size of commercial and industrial ventures. Phenomenal expansion has been actualised since the rise of modern technology, but the expansion in size does not necessarily mean a radical change in the character and the complexion of the corporate organisation. Islam recognises various kinds of partnership between two or more persons in commercial and industrial ventures :

(*a*) *Al-Muḍārabah* (المضاربه) or *al-Muqāraḍah* (المقارضه) : partnership between capital on one side and personal effort on the other. The proportionate share in the profits is determined by mutual agreement. But the losses, if any, are to be borne by the owner of the capital alone. The manager may also contribute to the capital. In that case he shall have a dual capacity in the partnership as a capitalist and as a manager. If there are two or more persons on the side of management, their share need not be equal ; it may vary in consideration of the prestige, reputation for business acumen and reliability enjoyed by each.

(*b*) *Shirkat al-'Inān* (شركة العنان) : patnership in both capital and labour. Two or more persons invest their capital and work together for its exploitation. Both of them have an obligation to put in actual work personally. The profit is to be divided according to the percentage ratio agreed upon, while each one of them bears a share in the loss proportional to one's investment.

(*c*) *Shirkat al-'Abdān* (شركة الابدان) : partnership between two or more persons in skill and mental and/or physical labour only (without capital). It may be called an association by workers and labourers for production. All the associates need not do the same job, practise the same skill or belong to the same profession. Each one of them shall have such proportionate share in the profits as is mutually agreed upon among them. Naturally the share in the profits will be in consideration of the importance of the job performed by each.

(*d*) *Shirkat al-Wujūh* (شركة الوجوه) : partnership between two or more persons carrying on business on credit alone (without investment of capital). In this Credit Partnership the capital of the parties consists not of cash or merchandise but entirely of credit. It is quite probable that persons of known integrity and business acumen take commodities on credit and dispose them of profitably with their efforts. Such partners will share the possession of the commodities taken on credit in a ratio mutually agreed upon among them. They will also share the profits in a ratio mutually agreed upon, which need not necessarily correspond to their share in the possession of the commodities. But their share in the losses will correspond to their share in the ownership of the commodities. This is because the share in the possession of the commodities obtained on credit stands for the share in the capital. In this regard the general principle is that "the profit be divided as agreed upon between the contracting parties, their liability being in proportion to their share in the capital."[20]

It may be noted that in the present context credit only means the faith of the people in the capacity of a person to clear the dues faithfully and on time. Quite possibly such confidence may be enjoyed by a person of meagre resources and humble status in

20. *Vide* the saying of the Prophet quoted in ***Hidāyah***, "K. at-Shirkah":
"الربح على ما شرط العاقدان و الوضيعة على قدر المالين"
Sometimes the saying is ascribed to 'Alī instead of the Prophet.

society. On the other hand, a personage of rank and wealth may not enjoy the same confidence. The common practice these days of associating influential persons with commercial firms for the promotion of business has no sanction in Islam. Such influential-persons who contribute nothing either in capital or management/labour are not entitled to any share in the profits. Obviously their influence is only a source of corruption.

Similarly, the association with a commercial firm of some national of a country where foreigners are debarred from business (as in Saudi Arabia and Kuwait) merely for the sake of obtaining trade licences in his name is immoral and unlawful in Islam. Such a person is not entitled to any share in the profits just for lending his name to the enterprise.

(e) *Shirkat al-Mufāwaḍah* (شركة المفاوضة): a partnership embracing all monetary resources of the parties to the contract, in an equal manner and involving mutual agency (وكالة) and suretyship (كفالة) on the part of all the partners.

It is remarkable that a study of the above provisions of *Fiqh* has led Abraham L. Udovitch of the Princeton University to make the following important observation :

Until forty years ago the prevalent view was that the Middle Ages constituted a pre-credit era. . . . The earliest Muslim legal sources now justify the assertion that already in the eighth century, and possibly earlier, credit arrangements of various types constituted an important feature of both trade and industry. . . . Any assertion that mediaeval credit was used for consumption only, and not for production, is quite untenable with reference to the mediaeval Near East.[21]

Corporations. Corporations play an important role in modern economy. This is a new development. In the eighteenth-

21. *JAOS*, Vol. LXXXVII (1967), No. 3.

century Europe "the investor, the person looking to a return in the way of interest only, had little to do with business; his investments were in land or in public funds. The business man borrowed occasionally from banks or professional money-lenders but had no permanent associates divorced from the management". Later on the corporation emerged as "an association of a considerable number of persons, strangers to each other and generally investors not closely concerned with the management". It is characterised by continuing existence, inactive members and limitation of liability. There is a clear separation between owners and managers : a large number of share-holders with directors selected from among them and managers chosen by the directors.

In the olden days of Islam the capital-owners always sought the partnership of those who possessed managerial skill The investors were not shy of taking risks; they could not look to a return in the way of interest only. Hence Islam does not envisage an association of investors, strangers among themselves and offering their shares of the capital to a legal personality like the corporation. Islam only visualises the owner advancing the capital to a real person. It is quite reasonable to believe that Islam aims at ensuring the active interest of both the capital-owners and the managers in the enterprise. It is a fact that "the sense of association for common ends has virtually disappeared among the share-holders of the modern corporation". The notion of a joint venture for common profit or common loss is non-existent. The ease of transfer encourages desertion of the venture in case of expected loss as a rat deserts a sinking ship and a rush upon shares when the going is easy and profitable. This further results in a vast deal of unproductive effort in the way of stock gambling. The people these days have ceased to think over points of morality involved in these transactions. Nevertheless, it is not easy to assert that there is no debit side to the social gain, if any. As for Islam no gain is a gain unless it is morally unassailable.

When all is said, the continuity of existence and operation and the easy supply of means for any undertaking, however large, stand out as the most prized benefits of the modern corporation. Obviously, the partnerships of the kind known to, and recognised by, Islam in the past are wound up with the death of any partner and, the number of active partners known to each other being small, the supply of resources is also comparatively limited. The Muslim legists are only obsessed with *ribā*. They are prone to declare the corporation lawful just because the dividend, as distinguished from a fixed rate of interest, is lawful. They do not bother about examining the detailed constitution and working of the corporation. Anyway, many of them are prone to argue the admissibility of the corporations in Islam. It is made out that there is a kind of two-party agreement between the general body of share-holders and the directors to run the enterprise with the services of the managers. This would be plausible only if the directors represented the share-holders and not the shares, i.e. if they were elected on the basis of one vote for each share-holder irrespective of the number of shares held by him.

Even then the directors represent only the party of owners; the other party of managers is no party to the agreement on the enterprise. The manager is just a paid employee of the capital-owners. The standard rules of Islam demand that it should be an agreement between two distinct parties of the capital-owners and the managers and that both the parties should actively and personally promote a definite enterprise. Obviously the modern corporation is not a partnership between the owners of the capital (مال) and the person/s (بدن) undertaking the management of a definite enterprise by virtue of the confidence reposed in him/

them by the investors. It is at best an association of the capital-owners who would remain inactive and uncommitted through the vicissitudes of profit and loss and choose a few from among themselves to direct an enterprise with the services of a hired manager.[22] It is a matter of *ijtihād* whether the deviation from the standard form conflicts in any way with the spirit of social justice in Islam.

One thing is certain that if the standard form of Islam is adhered to, managerial skill will be at a high premium. It is much more honourable and just for the managers to be partners in the enterprise than to be paid employees of the capital-owners. It is now universally recognised that the managers deserve not wages (fixed salary) but a share in the profits. Hence considerable resort is made to profit-sharing arrangements such as *tantieme* and bonus.

Co-operative Societies. The constitution of the co-operative societies also fails to satisfy the condition that the manager or the person who is trusted to operate the enterprise personally should be a partner—a party to the agreement between him and the capital-owners—and not a paid employee of a mere legal personality. Further, the division of the profits according to the volume of transactions—purchases or products—is also against the recognised principle of Islam that the dividend be determined according to the contribution to the capital or the labour involved in running the concern.

We have all the time to bear in mind the definition of a *shirkat* in Islam: it is a contract between two or more persons who launch upon a financial enterprise for the sake of profits. In

22. The above points have been very ably set out by the modern scholar, Taqī al-Dīn al Nabhānī in his book: *al-Nizām al-'Iqtiṣādiy fi al-'Islām.* They merit serious attention as pointers to the way of reform in the constitution of a corporation so as to turn it into a *partnership* between the investors and the managers.

the basic notion two "persons"—responsible men of flesh and blood—loom large: the capital-owner and the manager. If the person (بدن) of the manager as a partner is not in the picture, just one single party of capital-owners cannot make a *shirkat*.

Manufacturing and Industrial Plants. Industry is not a new phenomenon; only it has grown in size and sophistication. So long as the essential nature of an economic activity remains unchanged, the broad principles of the Sharī'ah continue to apply to it irrespective of the stage of development reached by it. For example, industrial plants for the manufacture of textiles and swords are known to have existed in the time of the Prophet. The character of an industrial plant is determined by the material manufactured by it. A brewery cannot by owned by a Muslim because its product, namely, wine, is unlawful for him Of course, a non Muslim can own it. All the plants which turn out items of private ownership, such as shoes and textiles, remain the private property of the owner/s. There is no question of their being nationalised and taken over by the State. Whatever is allowed to pass into private ownership is secure against forcible take-over by the State. On the other hand, industries for processing and refining raw mineral deposits—such as petrol, gas, iron, gold, salt and coal—are of necessity Public Property. It has already been established that the imponderable and inexhaustible gifts of Nature cannot pass into private ownership. It follows that the industries for processing and refining them should also be kept out of the private sector. Otherwise the owner/s of the processing industries would be in a position to deprive the people of FREE gifts of Nature by charging rent for them. That is to say, the processors would be tempted to impose a price in excess of the expenditure involved in processing, thus laying the base for the exploitation of the people. So there is no question of such industries passing into private hands. But it is worth remembering that public management is also under an obligation to ensure that the gifts of Nature remain FREE for the people. The State or public management is to run these industries on a no-profit-no-loss basis.

Nationalisation. The justification for nationalisation lies in illegitimate profits on the part of private owners. In Islam the illegitimate profits are stopped at source. So far as industries in the private sector are concerned, free competition in an open market is the only effective safeguard against illegitimate gains by the owners. This is ensured by outlawing all controls and restrictions on prices, currency, exchange and trade.[23] Thus the question of nationalisation does not arise at all. Of course, defence considerations have a priority over all the normal rights and privileges of the citizens. All the industries vital for defence are to be initiated and maintained, even commandeered outright and run, by the State or run by private owners according to the directives of the State in the public interest.

23. See next chapter.

Chapter III

PRICE, CURRENCY AND TRADE

Price Adjustment. A sound mechanism of price adjustment is all important for economic justice. The value of commodities and services consists in their utility for the satisfaction of human needs and desires. It will be remembered that in Islam certain commodities and services are declared "devoid of value" just as certain needs and desires are branded as false and unlawful. Barring those few exceptions, the value of all the commodities and services is priced in terms of currency at a level reached by the free operation of the natural law of supply and demand in the open market at any time. Thus the essential conditions of a sound self-operating mechanism of price adjustment are as follows: (1) No corner market; (2) No hoarding of gold and silver; (3) No price control; (4) No restrictions on trade; (5) Maintenance of gold standard.

(1) *No Corner Market*

The hoarding and corner marketing (*al-'iḥtikār* =الاحتكار) of commodities of any kind, particularly foodstuffs, with a view to creating an artificial scarcity and rise in prices is prohibited. The Prophet is reported to have said: "It is only a sinner who indulges in *'iḥtikār*."[1] Further, all methods of creating an artificial rise in prices are condemned in the severest terms. "Who-

1. Muslim and 'Abū Dāwūd, "Kitāb-al-Buyū'":

"لا يحتكر الا خاطئ" -

"من احتكر يريد ان يتغالى بها على المسلمين فهو خاطئ و قد برئت منه ذمة الله" -

ever meddles in any rates so as to raise them to the detriment of the Muslims he will deserve that Allah put him into a thick fire on the Day of Judgment."[2] A familiar method was for an uninterested third person to raise the price of a commodity in the presence of an intending buyer so as to dupe him. This is called "al-Najash" (النجش) and is expressly prohibited.[3] Similarly, the practice of the clever brokers rushing to the points of entry into the town and buying up the commodities cheap from the unsophisticated villagers in order to reap inflated middleman's profits is condemned. The Prophet ordered that the supplies be brought down to the market so that both the suppliers and the consumers may benefit from the natural level of prices.[4]

(2) *No* Kanz

The *kanz* or hoarding of surplus wealth in gold and silver is condemned in the severest terms:

And there are those who bury gold and silver and spend it not in the Way of Allah: announce unto them a most grievous penalty —on the Day when heat will be produced out of that (wealth) in the fire of Hell, and with it will be branded their foreheads, their flanks, and their backs.—"This is the (treasure) which ye buried for yourselves: taste ye, then, the (treasures) ye buried"! (Qur., ix. 34-35).

2. 'Abū Dawūd al-Ṭayālisī :

"من دخل فى شئ من أسعار المسلمين ليغليه عليهم كان حقا على الله ان يقعده بعظم من النار يوم القيامة" -

3. Al-Tirmidhī, "Abwāb al-Buyū' " : لا تناجشوا.

4. Ibid :

"لا يبيع حاضر لباد و دعوا الناس يرزق الله بعضهم من بعض" -

Ahmad, *Musnad*, II, 63 :

"عن ابن عمر ان النبى (صلعم) نهى عن تلقى السلع حتى يهبط بها الأسواق و نهى عن النجش و قال لا يبيع بعضكم على بعض" -

This important aspect of the economic system of Islam was highligted by 'Abū Dharr's interpretation of the above *'Āyat* in the context of the conditions which prevailed during the reign of 'Uthmān.

'Abū Dharr would not allow surplus wealth to be hoarded in gold and silver. He maintained that it was not enough to pay the obligatory *Zakāt*. "The *Zakāt*-payer should not stop at it"; he had other obligations too.[5] He should participate with all his surplus wealth in acts of public welfare, beginning, of course, with his neighbours, relations and friends. 'Abū Dharr would not object to surplus wealth being invested in lawful productive enterprise, nor did he actually mean that nobody be allowed to collect and save money for the satisfaction of his needs within the limit prescribed in the Sharī'ah. This is in line with the distinction made out by modern economists between hoarding and saving. By "hoarding" is meant the putting aside of money (or jewels and the like, easily convertible into money and easily stored) with no expectation and intention of using them either for investment or for expenditure on consumer's goods. "Saving is the putting aside of money with an eye to its use within a not distant time.[6] *Kanz* is the Qur'ānic term for "hoarding," while *'iddikhār* (ادخار) is the Arabic equivalent of "saving". 'Abū Dharr was quite clear and emphatic that, even though the *Zakāt* be paid, the hoarding of surplus wealth (in gold and silver) was unlawful.

Wealth earned and owned by individuals may be a blessing or a curse for the community. Of course, the satisfaction of one's legitimate needs is the first charge on one's lawfully earned

5. Tirmidhī, "Kitāb al-Zakāt":
"عن فاطمة بنت قيس قالت سمعت النبى (صلعم) يقول : ان فى أموالكم حقا سوى الزكوة" .

6. Taussig, *Principles of Economics*, I, 74.

income ; there is no conceivable objection to it. Moreover, spending on one's personal needs confers benefits on the community as a whole inasmuch as it sets the money in circulation. It is only the hoarding of surplus wealth which makes all the difference. In any case, it blocks the money and withdraws it from circulation, which affects adversely the volume and the pace of economic activity and the natural process of circulation and wide distribution of wealth. The crucial point is that the payment of the obligatory *Zakāt* does not mitigate the anti-social consequences of hoarding. It will be remembered that Islam does not countence any use for gold and silver except as currrency or medium of exchange. The prohibition of the use of golden or silver ware is accounted for by the same considerations of economic welfare and social justice. Very reluctantly, and I should say quite sparingly, a concession was made to feminine nature in permitting the wearing of ornaments. It is specifically in respect of ornaments that 'Umm Salamah clearly asked the Prophet : Do they constitute *kanz* ("hoarding" as mentioned in the *'ayal al-kayy* above) ? The Prophet replied : If they are in such quantity that *Zakāt* is levied on them and the same is paid, then they are excluded from *kanz*. This particular exception does not warrant total abrogation of the clear words of *'āyal al-kayy*.[7]

(3) *No Price Control*

Price control by State authorities is ruled out in absolute terms :

روى أنس قال : غلا السعر على عهد النبى (صلعم) فقالوا : يا رسول الله ! لو سعرت لنا ، فقال : ان الله هوالقابض الرازق الباسط المسعر ، و انى لا'رجوأن القى الله ولايطالبنى أحد بمظلمة ظلمتها اياه فى دم ولا مال (رواه ابو داؤد و الترمذى و صححه) -

7. See my *Studies in Islamic History and Culture*, Chapter VI.

روى أبو داؤد وغيره حديث العلاء بن عبد الرحمان عن أبيه عن أبى هريرة (رض) قال : جاء رجل الى رسول الله (صلعم) فقال : يا رسول الله ! سعر لنا ، فقال : بل ادعوا الله ، ثم جاءه رجل فقال : يا رسول الله سعر لنا ، فقال : بل الله يرفع و يخفض ، و انى لأرجو أن القى الله وليست لأحد عندى مظلمة ـ

"It is Allah Who raises or lowers the prices," i.e. no interference or control by a human agency should tamper in any way with the operation of the natural law of supply and demand. Occasional shortages of particular commodities are due to hoarding or exhaustion of stocks. It is the duty of the State to break the hoarding and to arrange for supplies from all possible sources. 'Umar did the same to relieve the distress caused by soaring prices of food in Medina; he brought in supplies from Egypt and Syria and the prices went down the natural way.

(4) *No Restrictions on Trade*

In regard to foreign trade, Islam visualises free movement of goods throughout the world without any initial prejudice on nationalist ground. This is essential for the untampered and unhampered operation of the law of supply and demand in the framework of open competition on a worldwide basis. The freedom of trade is complementary to the freedom from exchange control and from currency management. As a matter of fact, all the freedoms are interlinked. Freedom of internal trade is just a part of the freedom of external trade. Again, the absence of any distinction on religious ground is to be observed here as in the whole field of economics. Every national of an Islamic State—a Muslim as well as a *dhimmī*—has the right—a fundamental right—of free import and export subject only to the following considerations of strategy and defence.

(*i*) The export of war material—all such material as increases the war potential of an enemy State (*dār al-ḥarb*)—is banned. But, apart from this, there is no other restriction on trade with an enemy State. It is recalled in this connection that the Prophet exhorted Thumāmah to supply provisions to the people of Mecca, who were declared enemies at the time. Also the Muslim merchants maintained trade relations with enemy States in the days of the *Ṣaḥābah* without incurring any kind of disapproval.

The particulars of the cases cited above are as follows :

(*a*) Thumāmah ibn 'Uthāl was a chieftain of Yamāmah. Early in 6 H., he was taken prisoner by a Muslim detachment, and brought to Medina. Here the gentle treatment of the Prophet impressed him so much that he embraced Islam. On return journey, he passed through Mecca and heard some abusive cuts on his conversion. He said : Not a grain of Yamāmah can now be imported into your city, unless the Prophet directs otherwise. A famine is said, consequently, to have ensued in Mecca. When the Meccans were reduced to great straits on that account, they besought the Prophet to lift the ban on their foodstuff and cloths (ميرة), which was graciously conceded.

(*b*) The Prophet himself once sent a quantity of the dates of Medina to the Meccan magnate, 'Abū Sufyān, and required in return hides. This is said to have occurred at a time when hostilities were continuing between Mecca and Medina.[8]

(*c*) There is a State document of the time of the Prophet, in which trade with the enemy was expressly permitted :

With the name of God, the Most Merciful, the All-Merciful.

This is the writ of protection from God and Muḥammad, the Prophet and Messenger of God, in favour of Yuḥannah ibn Ru'bah (John son of Rubin) and the people of Ailah.

Their boats and their traders on land and sea shall have the

8. Dr M. Hamidullah, *The Muslim Conduct of State* (Lahore 1 68, Sh. Muhammad Ashraf), paras 392-3.

protection of God and of Muḥammad, the Prophet. This includes also the people of Syria, of Yaman, of countries beyond the seas (أهل البحر) who are with them (i.e. the people of Ailah).

It is to be noted that Ailah (modern 'Aqabah, on the Red Sea) was subdued and annexed by the Prophet during the expedition of Tabūk, in the year 9 H., when he had set out against the Byzantines. This could not prevent him from permitting his vassal to trade with the enemy.[9]

From the above examples, Dr Ḥamīdullah concludes that "it rests wholly and solely with the Muslim government whether and to what extent to permit its subjects and those under its jurisdiction to trade with a belligerent State. And Muslim jurists seem to side with those who opine that everything is permitted unless prohibited. There is no reason to exclude trade from this all-embracing rule." [10]

(*ii*) In the case of those States which have a treaty of peace with the Islamic State, the terms of the trade will be governed by the provisions of the treaty. In the absence of any provision to the contrary, the trade will be free. As far as possible, no obstacles will be put in the way of the natural flow of goods and services. Of course, the ban on the export of war material will apply in every case.

(*iii*) Customs duty, in so far as it is levied, has a reference to the merchant and not the merchandise. If the merchant is a national of an Islamic State—a Muslim or a *dhimmī*—he is not liable to any import or export duty whatsoever.[11]

9. Ibid., paras 547-8.
10. Ibid., para 540.
11. 'Abū 'Ubaid, *al-Amwāl*, No. 1633 :

عن ابراهيم بن مهاجر قال : سمعت زياد بن حدير يقول : "أنا أول عاشر عشر فى الاسلام" قلت : من كنتم تعشرون ؟ قال : ما كنا نعشر مسلما ولا معاهدا ، كنا نعشر نصارى بنى تغلب .

(*iv*) All octroi and excise duties are condemned in the severest terms: "He who levies *maks* (sales tax) shall not enter the Paradise," said the Prophet.[12] 'Umar II abolished the *maks* saying it was tantamount to *bakhs* which is mentioned in the following verse of the Qur'ān:

And O people! give just measure and weight, nor withhold (*bakhs*) from the people the things that are their due: commit no evil in the land with intent to do mischief (xi. 85).[13]

(*v*) As for the nationals of an enemy State, the Islamic State is permitted (not obliged) to treat them on a reciprocal basis, i.e. to charge on their consignments such duty (but nothing in excess of it) as the enemy State charges on the consignments of the nationals of the Islamic State. It is clear that the intention is to discourage the other States from charging customs duty and not to relish it as a trade barrier or a source of revenue.

(5) *Maintenance of Gold Standard*

Goods and services are produced either individually or corporately. The producer is free to exchange them for the goods and services offered by another producer within the country or out-

12. Ibid., No. 1624 :

عن عقبة بن عامر انه سمع رسول الله (صلعم) يقول : لايدخل الجنة صاحب مكس -

13. Ibid., No. 1628 :

كتب عمر بن عبد العزيز الى عدى بن أرطاة "- - - وضع عن الناس المكس ، و ليس بالمكس ، ولكنه البخس الذى قال الله تعالى : " - - - ولا تبخسوا الناس أشياء هم ولا تعثوا فى الأرض مفسدين" -

Vide also No. 1638 :

قال أبو عبيده : وجوه هذه الأحاديث التى ذكرنا فيها العاشر وكراهة المكس و التغليظ فيه أنه قد كان له أصل فى الجاهلية ، يفعله ملوك العرب و العجم جميعا ، فكانت سنتهم أن يأخذوا من التجار عشر أموالهم اذا مروا بها عليهم -

side. The government's function is to facilitate the exchange by certifying the currency and maintaining the gold standard unhesitatingly and ungrudgingly. The currency is then left free to find its own level in the world market. The interplay of natural factors contributes to the achievement of just equilibrium while control by any quarter whatsoever brings an undue advantage to one or the other class of people.

Currency. All the economists agree, as common sense would testify to it, that currency came into being as the result of man's growing need for a common medium of exchange. This common medium of exchange in its very nature must be a substance such as represents the actual labour of the person with whom it originates and is, therefore, acceptable on its own account. The intervention of government was never called forth to give a particular value to currency. Being a commodity in itself, the value of the currency is governed by the natural forces whose interplay determines the value of all the commodities in the world. All that the people needed the government to do for them was to certify the weight and the fineness of a particular piece of metal. Thus if man were to develop economy the natural way, he would never allow the government to arrogate to itself the power to give an artificial value to a particular piece of metal. The question of what is called the creation of money does not arise at all. Man has now had sufficient experience to learn that no private person or organisation can be trusted with the power to issue currency and he has also begun to distrust the government in this respect as shown by his insistence on a government-cum-private authority hedged round with certain statutory laws and legal restrictions. It is, however, really strange that man should have ever reconciled himself at all to the idea of creation of money out of nothing in any form, e.g. in the form of paper issue, without full reserve or extension of credit by the banks. The citizens of the Middle Ages were indeed more vigilant and more jealous of their rights when they stoutly refused to accept any paper or leather currency sought to be imposed by some of their autocratic sovereigns,[14] who, curiously enough, are so unsparingly denounced at a time when the entire world seems to have resigned itself to the scourge of fiduciary issue.

Islam regards money only as a token of labour; there can be no token unless there is the thing betokened. What a government can and, as a matter of fact, ought to do is to stimulate labour and the production of goods. The resulting increase in the number of transactions will create its own money. This is ensured by the conditions governing (*a*) production, (*b*) hoarding and (*c*) the use of precious metals. It is significant, though few people realise it, that gold and silver mines within the boundaries of the Islamic State are treated as the common property of the entire community to be worked in a way which would maintain throughout their character as a free gift of Nature. This means that the amount of gold produced will represent exactly the amount of labour expended. Then taxation under an Islamic State is to be not on the basis of "income" as we have it almost everywhere in the present day but on the basis of "hoarding year after year". This principle has the remarkable effect of preserving the incentive to greater and more efficient work and at the same time directing the continuous flow of all savings, without there being any idle capital, into productive and profitable channels. Further, there is

14. The issue of leather notes is ascribed to 'Umar and to Humāyūn, the king of India (Dr Yūsufuddīn, *Islām ke Ma'āshī Naẓariyye*, II, 494-5). Perhaps 'Umar's notes were only a kind of cheque Paper money called "chao" (چاو) was issued in 693/1294 by Ṣāḥib Dīwān al-Mamālik, Ṣadruddīn 'Aḥmad al-Razzāq, who supervised the commissariat of the 'Īl-Khān Gaykhātū (Fischel, *Jews in the Economic and Political Life of Mediaeval Islam*, London : 1937, pp. 118-9).

the express prohibition against the use of the precious metals in arts. No Muslim can have any use for articles made of gold and silver and even ornaments for the adornment of women are permitted within limits though not altogether forbidden in consideration of a common failing in the weaker sex. It is really regrettable that the economic implications of these injunctions of Islam, which are generally regarded as signifying nothing but a sort of asceticism, puritanism and other-worldliness, are yet to be worked out for presentation to the modern world. This much, however, will be clear to anyone who cares to make a cursory study of the relevant chapters of *Fiqh* that Islam intended gold and silver to serve only and only as a medium of exchange. Hence the greatest possible stability is ensured; there can be no fluctuations in the value of the precious metals consequent on an increase or decrease in the demand for use in arts, which, by the way, is thoroughly anti-social, involving as it does the locking up of capital in idle fanciful productivity. Under such conditions any change in the value of money must represent greater or less output and efficiency of labour in the community. And such a change is of necessity gradual and real.

It will be seen that the system enjoined by Islam is characterised by unique simplicity and thorough automatism. It is simple enough to be clearly understood by the man-in-the-street, whose confidence is never allowed to be misused by any authority. The government is bound to discharge its function of certification with scrupulous honesty. The coins are to bear a face value exactly equal to the intrinsic worth of the metal contained in them, though it is permissible in certain cases to charge a small sum by way of seigniorage[15] as was actually done by 'Abd al-Malik, the

15. Even that small charge was abolished by 'Umar II. See 'Abū Yūsuf, *K. al-Kharāj*, p. 19.

Umayyad Caliph, reputed for his reforms in this sphere. Thus the standard gold and silver money will be the actual medium of exchange guaranteed against all tampering from any source. So far as paper money is concerned, it can be issued merely for the sake of convenience; hence the only form it can take is that of the American Gold Certificates. Any issue without full reserve is a gross betrayal of the ordinary man's confidence. The argument of economy in the use of gold that is sometimes advanced in favour of paper currency is on the face of it fallacious. So long as a Gold Certificate is in circulation the reserve behind it cannot be said to be idle. It is the gold itself that is actually in circulation, though the transfer is effected by means of a token. There can be no question of paper being used as currency on its own account without forgetting the fundamental truth that currency must be a substance representing so much actual labour. This "neutralising" of money also ensures automatism. Under such a system any fluctuations in the value of money, as of any commodity for the matter of that, will be subject to natural forces and not to the machinations of any person or persons. The functions of the government regarding money being reduced to the bare minimum of honest certification, it will be compelled to strike at the root causes of an economic deterioration, whenever there is any, instead of resorting to such sham devices as the management of currency, which, even when inspired by the best of motives, is as good as artificial respiration administered to a dying man.

It will be remembered that a good deal of the management of currency these days is designed to bolster up unsound economic systems. The simple currency laws of Islam as described above are to be viewed in the background of the entire economic fabric, the most salient feature of which is that exchange must always be scrupulously honest and that it must always represent ultimately an exchange of labour for labour. It is on this ground that Islam is irrevocably opposed to all kinds of interest and banking. Today when a banker raises a huge superstructure of 60% credit on the basis of mere 40% deposits, Western economists would say that it is only "risky"; there is nothing "immoral" about it. But such a thing is ruled outright in Islam. All kinds of stakes, gambling and lottery are also forbidden owing to the same consideration that the gain thereby does not represent so much actual labour. If this principle be observed as strictly as Islam enjoins in all dealings between man and man, then all the ramifications of the vicious process whereby the rich grow richer and the poor poorer are eliminated at source. Most of the economic ills of the present day are due to the same fact that very often money is forced out of the hands of one who has actual labour to his credit into the hands of one who has not.

Now the ways and means open to an Islamic State for coping with a war situation are voluntary help and straight open commandeering. Such a process has not yet become unfamiliar to the modern world and needs no explanation. It need only be remembered that an Islamic State subsists, not on the mere will of the bare majority of the people, but on the religious faith of the entire community. Hence it is in a most advantageous position to undertake the above measures without any fear of overt or covert resistance on the part of the people. It can very well be imagined that these honest straightforward measures leave no such aftermath as inflation is always bound to do both during and after the war. After all there is nothing wrong in the conscription and regimentation of the entire available resources by a popular government engaged in a total war. The immorality lies in the adoption of a method which reduces the whole affair to a legalised confidence trick, involving an unequal and injudicious distribution of the burden of sacrifice and leaving behind a legacy of unfair and inequitable appropriation of economic advantages by the idle few at the expense of the toiling millions.

The Gold Standard. Islam binds the government to scrupulous honesty in its task of certification of the weight and the fineness of the gold coin and in its promise to pay the equivalent in gold kept in reserve for the paper currency issued by it. This is, of course, the essence of the gold standard. Further, by restraining the government from controlling exchange and foreign trade (except to the extent required by the interests of defence) Islam ensures full convertibility and free export of gold to other countries, Muslim as well as non-Muslim. The monetary system of Islam is characterised by perfect sensitiveness. The most important result that follows from the above is the stabilisation of foreign exchange and of the price level. Also the danger of over-issue, which is the worst form of fraud and deceit by the law-enforcing authority, is eliminated at source.

It is also important to note that Islam prohibits the exchange of one gold coin with another except at the par value of the gold content of each of them. The usual money-changer's discount is unlawful:

The Prophet said: "A dīnār for a dīnār and a dirham for a dirham (at par) without any excess as between them." [16]

If the implications of this simple dictum were fully realised by all the units participating in international trade and monetary exchange, they would eventually agree on a universal currency of a fixed gold content, which will be a boon to the humanity at large.[17] Such a consummation would be a guarantee of economic

16 - ''الدينار بالدينار والدرهم بالدرهم ، لا فضل بينهما'' ۔

17. Dr Muḥammad Yūsufuddīn, op. cit., II, 496-7.

justice and freedom as between the nations. By contrast, the present-day international agencies (which stand at the apex of governmental controls at every stage of economic activity) such as the International Monetary Fund are merely the instruments of maintaining the hegemony of the developed countries and imposing economic thraldom on the developing countries. All the evils arising from controls such as smuggling will be unknown under the free, simple and honest exchange stipulated above. It will generate the fullest confidence of the traders in an adequate return for their goods and services, promoting unlimited expansion of economic activity and exchange on a universal scale. The unreasonable fear of the gold drain is one of the superstitions of modern economics. It is unreasonable because each national State wants to buy from others without paying in specie which is valuable to the seller. It is just the ordinary man's awkward selfishness and greed, if not deceit and predation, which is magnified and practised on a national scale. The gain in goods and services is always equal to the payments in gold. If such payments were a drain and a loss, then all mercantile transactions are a loss for the buyer. The total exports of a country are to be set off against its total imports just as the total expenses of an individual are necessarily to match the total of goods and services acquired by him. How true that "the flow of specie is an indicator of the currents of international trade, not in itself a matter of serious importance. And in the main it takes care of itself, ceasing by a quasi-automatic process when the needed readjustment of imports and exports has been accomplished."[18]

18. Taussig, op. cit., I, 449.

Chapter IV

THE CONSUMPTION AND DISTRIBUTION OF WEALTH

(1) *Personal Expenditure*

Lawful needs are of two kinds: (*a*) basic minimum common to each and every individual and (*b*) extra comforts and amenities—ways of enjoyable elegant living—attained by the specially gifted members of the society. These are generally called "necessities" (the provision of which is the primary responsibility of the State) and "luxuries". I have deliberately avoided the word "luxuries" because of its bad association in un-Islamic societies. In Islam unlawful luxuries are no luxuries; they are just "prohibitions". The so-called luxuries, if lawful, are *ṭayyibāt* (طيبات) and have no odium attaching to them. Islam envisages continuously progressive improvement in the means of production and consequently in the quality and quantity of products of all kinds. Now if there were the least odium attaching to the utilisation and enjoymen of these finer and more abundant products, it would result eithe in disregard of the odium or in slowing down the technological progress and dampening the economic activity. Therefore, Islam adopts the fully consistent and logical position that the fruits of technology and skilful production be available for enjoyment to those who can afford them.

Islam's prohibition of *'isrāf* (اسراف) and *tabdhīr* (تبذير) is as widely known as it is misunderstood. Both the Arabic words are technical terms with a special meaning in the dictionary of Islam. Their definition is to be sought from a careful study of the relevant canonical texts put in their proper context. Literally, *'isrāf* means "exceeding with respect to quantity in expenditure, which is ignorance of the values of the right objects," while *tabdhīr* means "exceeding in respect of the right objects of expenditure" (Lane). Technically, both the terms signify expending on items which are banned and prohibited, "expending otherwise than in obedience of God, whether little or much". Obviously the use of money in committing sins is a sin in itself. Thus a single dollar spent on wine is *'isrāf* and *tabdhīr*. But any amount spent on a spacious and comfortable house, a good car and a private helicopter is not *'isrāf/tabdhīr* in any way, provided the income is lawful. The opposite of *'isrāf/tabdhīr* is not *zuhd/taqashshuf* (زهد/تقشف), i.e. austerity ; rather it is *bukhl* (بخل), which technically means withholding money from obligatory, approved and lawful pursuits (*ḥaqq*=حق) within limits of permission (*mubāḥāt*=مباحات) and meritorious conduct (*ṭā'āt*=طاعات). The Qur'ān says :

Make not thy hand tied (like a niggard's) to thy neck, nor stretch it forth to its utmost reach, so that thou become blameworthy and destitute (xvii. 29).

In the above *'āyat* the latter prohibition applies to indiscriminate expending and not to large expending within permissible limits.

Those who, when they spend, are not extravagant and not niggardly, but hold a just (balance) between those (extremes) (xxv. 67).

Here also the point is made out that no money be spent on prohibited things (*ḥarām*=حرام) and no money be withheld from approved and lawful (*ḥalāl*=حلال) pursuits. It refers only to the quality of the acts, which is estimated without any reference to the amount of money involved.

If a thing is permitted, it is permitted irrespective of the cost involved. It will be a contradiction in terms to say that a thing is permissible in itself but prohibited because of the high cost involved. Moreover, high cost is a relative term. In underdeveloped societies anything beyond the bare necessities is regarded as costly and beyond the reach of the average man. With the rise in the standard of living in developed societies many amenities and comforts such as a refrigerator and a car come to be regarded as common amenities possessed by the average man. Of course, the rules of the Sharī'ah do not vary from society to society and from place to place. The Prophet is quite explicit on the point that "no part of your wealth really belongs to you except that which you ate and consumed, wore and wore out, and gave away (in charity) and stored (the benefit thereof)."[1] That is to say, obtain satisfaction from your wealth or give it away to others. If a man parts with his money in favour of a fellow human being, it is charity and not austerity. If a man can afford an amenity and would forgo it just to save money and keep it with himself, that is austerity. This austerity is a bad quality of heart. From the economic point of view, it is an attempt to clog the wheels of progress. It is not in vain that the Prophet took care to drive home the point that "Allah likes the effect of His bounty to be seen about His servant."[2]

Islam has only decried *taraf* (ترف), which signifies pride, arrogance and disregard for proper rules of conduct caused by possession and enjoyment of worldly riches :

1. *Mishkāt*, p. 440 :

هل لک من مالک "الا ما أكلت فأفنيت ، او لبست فأبليت ، او تصدقت فأمضيت" -

2. Al-Tirmidhī, "Abwāb al-Ādāb" :

"ان الله يحب أن يرى أثر نعمته على عبده" -

Never did We send a warner to a population, but the wealthy ones among them said: "We believe not in the (Message) with which ye have been sent" (xxxiv. 34).

But the wrongdoers pursued the enjoyment of the good things of life which were given them, and persisted in sin (xi. 116).

When We decide to destroy a population, We (first) send a definite order to those among them who are given the good things of this life and yet transgress; so that the word is proved true against them: then (it is) We destroy them utterly (xvii. 16).

All the above verses confirm that *taraf* has the sense of pride and haughty disobedience. The *mutrafīn* (مترفين) who were punished were punished for their denial of the message, their improper conduct, their *fisq* and not for their enjoyment of the amenities of life. *Taraf* is to be contrasted with *rafāh* (رفاه), which is enjoyment of comforts and amenities with humility and obedience to God. The Prophet has promised Divine Pleasure for the enjoyment of worldly riches in a spirit of humble piety. [3] It is also the duty of each one of us to provide as much comforts and amenities for one's dependants as one can afford:

Let the man of means spend according to his means (lxv. 7).

If a person does not make proper use of his money and just holds it with him, he is guilty of *bukhl* and liable to punishment for the same.[4] Money withheld on the plea of austerity is money withdrawn from circulation. A sound economic system is that which has a built-in device to pump the money back to the workers out of the coffers of the rich. Islam shows the way by encouraging better living albeit within lawful limits.

3. *Vide* al-Nabhānī, *al-Niẓām al-'Iqtiṣādiy*, p. 53; also 'Abd al-'Azīz al-Badrīy, *Ḥukm al-'Islām fi al-'Ishtirākiyyah* (Baghdad: 1962), p. 32. *'Irfāh* has been used in a bad sense in the context of excessive grooming and eating (*Lisān* RFH).

4. The Qur'ān, iii. 180; iv. 37.

(2) *The Eradication of Faqr*

Faqr (فقر) is not a relative term. In Islam it has a fixed and definite sense of deprivation—lack or satisfaction—of the basic needs of life (food, clothing and housing). It is significant that a *faqīr* is described as one whose basic needs are unsatisfied, but who would not beg of anyone.[5] The point is that it is the duty of the society and the State to attend to "want" and alleviate distress before there is a demand and a clamour for it, before it develops into class-consciousness and ends in class-hatred and class-war. It is sheer foolhardiness to repeat *ad nauseum* that there is no room for class-war in Islam while the society and the State remain criminally obliviou of the want and distress breeding in their bosom. Of course, Islam does not guarantee the health of one who exposes himself to contagion and lives in unhealthy surroundings. The revengeful ideologies, like that of communism, grow only in societies which refuse or neglect for long their responsibility for the satisfaction of the basic needs of each individual. The essence of social and economic justice is the acceptance by the society, through the agency of the State, of its collective responsibility to look after the satisfaction of the basic needs of each individual including, of course, the disabled, the decrepit and the handicapped one. Let us call it *al-takāful* (التكافل), i.e. collective social security, or *ḍamān al-'aysh* (ضمان العيش), i.e. collective economic welfare. A rose called by any other name would smell as sweet. In Islam this collective responsibility is undertaken and scrupulously discharged as an obligation to Allah. It will be

5. Muslim, "al-Naby 'an al-Mas'alah" :

عن أبى هريرة ان رسول الله قال : انما المسكين المتعفف ، اقرءوا ان شئتم "لا يسألون الناس الحافا" -

'Abū 'Ubaid, *al-Amwāl*, No. 1942 ; see also ibid., Nos. 1943, 1945 :

عن مجاهد قال : الفقير الذى لا يسأل و المسكين الذى يسأل " -

admitted on all hands that there is nothing inherent about it which might require godlessness as a precondition of it. It is much to be regretted that in modern times Islam has failed to project economic justice as the hallmark of a religious society.

(3) *Ways of Ensuring Basic Necessities*

The simple and practical ways of ensuring the basic necessities of life for each member of the society are as follows :

(*a*) When a person is unable to earn enough to satisfy his basic needs either temporarily or permanently, it is the moral duty of his near relatives (entitled to a share in his legacy) to render support to him.

(*b*) If the relatives are not in a position to support him, the responsibility devolves upon the Bait al-Māl first under the head of *Zakāt* and then under the rest of the heads.

(*c*) If there were not enough funds in the Bail al-Māl, the State shall resort to taxing the rich for the specific purpose in accordance with the needs of the situation The Qur'ān has laid down the general principle that wealth should not lie concentrated in the hands of the rich[6] and the Prophet has clearly said that there are obligations in respect of wealth over and above the *Zakāt*.[7]

The relations (potential inheritors) and the rich who are taxed for the benefit of their less fortunate members of the family or the community shall not be put to any inconvenience on that account. In the words of the Prophet : The best charity is that which proceeds from full satisfaction.[8] Here "full satisfaction" refers to the satisfaction of the desires and comforts normally

6. lix. 4.
7. Al-Tirmidhī : ان فى المال لحقاً سوى الزكواة
8. Bukhārī : خير الصدقة ما كان عن ظهر غنى و ابدأ بمن تعول

associated with the status of a person in society. The point is that the capacity for contribution to social welfare is determined not by the surplus over and above the satisfaction of one's basic needs of life; rather it is to be measured by the amount one is able to spare after enjoying the standard of living which is commonly enjoyed by men of one's rank and station in life. The satisfaction of the desires of one's own self and of the members of one's household is the first charge on one's earnings.[9] In no case should charity leave behind a sense of deprivation with the one who shows it for the sake of one's own moral elevation.

No convincing argument has yet been advanced to prove that the satisfaction of the basic needs of each individual can be achieved only by the dissolution of the institution of the family as a social and economic unit. On the other hand, man is far from being a machine; passions and sentiments form an important strand in the complex process of human motivation. Without love and sentimental attachment, the union of man and woman would be an inhuman affair. Experiments with modern nurseries have shown that hired mothering with scientific equipment is no substitute for genuine mother's love. Just ask any inmate of a Home for the Aged in Britain how he feels about it. Is it enough that the son is taxed by the State to provide old-age pension to the father without the milk of human kindness? Islam takes a complete view of human nature and administers social justice the

9. Muslim, "Kitab al-Zakāt":

قال رسول الله (صلعم) : یابن آدم انک ان تبذل الفضل خیرلک ، و ان تمسکہ شرلک ، و لا تلام علی کفاف و ابدأ بمن تعول ، والید العلیا خیر من السفلی"۔

Also 'Aḥmad, *Musnad*, III, 305:

" اذا کان أحدکم فقراً فلیبدأ بنفسه ، فان فضل فعلی عیاله ، فان کان فضل فعلی قرابته" ۔

tender human way rather than the unkind, impersonal and mechanical way.

A French couple, both of them journalists with communist leanings, confessed to me that they found communism very difficult to percolate to the Islamic society. Their judgment was based on their experiences in the Egyptian countryside. As they told me, in the off season when there is no plucking of the cotton, one could often see an unemployed young lad lying day and night under the shade of a tree with apparently no means and no support to fall back upon. Yet the poor lad was able to get on for months together without succumbing to starvation. This is because every morning and evening a sparse meal would come to him from one or the other of the neighbouring huts. Following the dictum of the Prophet,[10] the people of a locality would regard it as their collective responsibility to see that no one suffered from hunger around them.

Of course, the true application of the idea of collective social responsibility is the elimination of unemployment and not the maintenance of the unemployed through unorganised private charity. Similarly, the misapplication of the charitable feeling is responsible for promoting beggary as a lucrative profession. In Spain the people would beat an able-bodied beggar on the streets. They understood better the meaning of organised social security. Anyhow, the acceptance of obligation on the part of the well-to-do members towards the less fortunate ones is the most precious asset for ensuring the satisfaction of the basic needs of each individual. In Islam the sense of obligation is so strong that it finds expression in unorganised, desultory and often petty help indiscriminately offered to the deserving as well as the undeserving.

10. 'Aḥmad, *Musnad*, chap. 'Ibn 'Umar:

أيما أهل عرصة أصبح فيهم امرؤ جائعا فقد برئت منهم ذمة الله -

This rendered the task of the State so much easier if and when it set about organising social security and ensuring basic necessities to each individual. But alas! the modern Muslim States are only preoccupied with increasing production and industrialisation.

(4) *Taxation*

Let us first analyse and enumerate the obligations of the State and then proceed to examine the resources sanctioned for the same.

(*a*) In Islam the administration of *Zakāt* is the most important obligation of the State. It is one of the most elaborate institutions based on repeated precepts in the Qur'ān, the details of which -e thoroughly specified in the Ḥadīth and confirmed by the actual practice (*Sunnah*) traceable to the Prophet. The exact manner of the levy and collection of *Zakāt* is left in no doubt. The *Zakāt* fund forms a separate head of deposits in the Bait al-Māl; under no circumstances it is to be mixed up with the deposits under the rest of the heads of revenue. The beneficiaries of the *Zakāt* fund fall into eight categories which are specified in the following verse of the Qur'ān:

> Alms (*ṣadaqāt*) [taxes coming from the Muslims] are for [1] the poor (*fuqarā'*) and [2] the needy (*masākīn*), and [3] those employed to administer the (funds); for [4] those whose hearts have been (recently) reconciled (to truth); for [5] those in bondage and [6] in the debt; [7] in the cause of Allah; and for [8] the wayfarers; (thus is it) ordained by Allah, and Allah is full of Knowledge and Wisdom (ix. 60).

Fāqīr: who has something but not enough for his needs, who would not ask for help. It also applies to a labourer out of job and an immigrant in need of rehabilitation.

Miskīn: who has nothing at all. "The very high authority of the Caliph 'Umar is there to support the view that the term meant the poor among the non-Muslim inhabitants of the Islamic State. The Semitic philology also confirms it ; for instance, in the famous Code of Hammurabi we come across the term *mushkino*, which there means a resident alien, very much akin to the *dhimmīs* of the later Muslim law."[11]

Fī sabīlillāhi (in the path of Allah) : *jihād*, which is always meant by the term in the Qur'ān in the context of spending money (*'infāq*).

'Ibn al-sabīl : a stranded traveller. It is a comprehensive term, which allows for the provision of as many facilities for the travellers as possible.

It is expressly prohibited that the *Zakāt* fund be diverted to any other head of expenditure. If the fund is not utilised, the surplus will go on accumulating and be reserved in the Bait al-Māl. The disbursement within the frame of the eight categories is at the discretion of the 'Imām.

Clearly the basic concept underlying the institution of *Zakāt* is the essential, inescapable obligation of the State to ensure the satisfaction of the basic needs of each individual. The obligation is absolute and preferential in the sense that if the collection at the normal rate is inadequate for the purpose the State is compelled to supplement the same by resorting to borrowing (of course, without interest) and/or taxation to the extent and till such time as is required by the needs of the situation.

(*b*) Of equal importance is the prime obligation of the State to provide for the needs of *jihād* in arms and equipment. This obligation is also unlimited by the funds available in the normal way. The charge is to be met from *Zakāt* as well as other sources of

11. Dr. M. Hamidullah, "Budgeting and Taxation in the Time of the Holy Prophet," *Journal of the Pakistan Historical Society*, Karachi, Vol. III (1955), p. 8.

income to the Bait al-Māl. If the needs are high, the funds are to be expanded by resort to borrowing and taxation.

(*c*) Obviously the State has to maintain an efficient civil, military and judicial administration. The civil servants, the military personnel and the members of the judiciary are to be paid reasonable salaries according to the nature of their work and the standards prevailing at the time. This charge is to be met with the income of the Bait al-Māl under heads other than those of *Zakāt*, the principal head earmarked for the same being that of the *Kharāj*.[12] This charge is also absolute and unavoidable. If the funds in the Bait al-Māl were not enough, it has to be met with borrowing and/or taxation.

Super-taxation for the needs of defence was actually resorted to on critical occasions in the history of Islam, for example, during the war waged by Quṭuz against the Tartar hordes. A *fatwā* in support of the new war tax imposed by the king of Egypt was issued by the famous doctor of religion, al-'Izz b. 'Abd al-Salām. Most of the authorities, such as al-Shāṭibī (*al-'I'tiṣām*, II, 104) and al-Ghazālī (*al-Mustaṣfā*, I, 303-94), concurred in the *fatwā*. But it is quite characteristic of Islamic society that resistance to the "innovation" was not altogether wanting.

(*d*) Public works—highways, water plants, mosques, hospitals and educational and training institutes—are to be set up at public expense for the utility and convenience of the common people. Even the *Zakāt* fund can be employed for promoting many of such schemes. But if the funds in the Bait al-Māl are not enough,

12. 'Abū 'Ubaid, op. cit., No. 737 :

"ان موضع الخراج الذى يوضع فيه سوى موضع العشر، انما ذلک فی أعطية المقاتلة و أرزاق الذرية (القضاة)"۔

'Abū Yūsuf, *al-Kharāj*, pp. 186-7 :

"لاتجر على الولاة والقضاة من مال الصدقة شيئا"۔

5

borrowing and taxation are to be resorted to within the limits of the easy taxpaying capacity of the people. It will be remembered that borrowing and taxation constitute the last unhappy resort for the provision of the basic needs and amenities of the people. Any extension and development of public works shall depend on the state of material prosperity in the community. It will also be recalled that education in particular has always thrived on public philanthropy in Islam.

(*e*) In an emergency as, for example, that arising out of a natural calamity, the State shall strain all the resources of the Bait al-Māl and the general public to meet the situation. In this connection it is most refreshing to recall the words of the Prophet : "Whenever the people of the tribe of 'Ash'ar run out of stocks in war or they exhaust their resources or the provisions for their dependants are depleted in Medina, they collect all that they have in one sheet of cloth and then divide it among them equally in uniform measure. So they are my people and I am one of them."[13]

It will be seen from the above that taxation is premissible within limits specifically for the discharge of the obligations laid upon the State. It follows that :

(*i*) All taxes are direct. Indirect taxes are simply ruled out inasmuch as they are designed to hoodwink the unwary public. The taxes should represent the conscious contribution of the people to a cause of public interest. The taxpayer is always called upon to make the contribution as a token of his concern for the common weal.

(*ii*) There is no taxation with the studied object of limiting

13. Muslim, "Bāb Faḍā'il al-'Ash'ariyyīn" (al-Maṭba'at al-Miṣrīyyah, 1349), XVI, 61-2 :

"ان الأشعريين اذا أرملوا فى الغزو و فنى زادهم أو قل طعام عيالهم بالمدينة جمعوا ما كان عندهم فى ثوب واحد ثم اقتسموه بينهم فى اناء واحد بالسوية فهم منى وأنا منهم" -

the legitimate earnings of the talented members of the community. It is enough to regulate the ways of investment and earning. Similarly, Death Duty is ruled out. Islam's elaborate law of inheritance is enough to sequester the fortune lawfully made by a person during his lifetime and left behind at his death. The fortune, however large it may be, is parcelled out among a large number of near and distant relations, male as well as female.[14] There is no room for the evils of primogeniture : no perpetual concentration of wealth in a single hand, no question of the wealth being squandered by a lone inheritor, who is often incompetent, indolent and indulgent in luxury. There is wide dispersion of prosperity among individuals who are provided with the means of promoting general economic activity. Chances of waste of unearned income are greatly reduced because of the large number of beneficiaries involved. It is the right of the owner to dispose of by will just one-third of his fortune without favouring any of the potential inheritors thereby. The purpose of common weal is amply served. Why should the State cast a covetous eye and encroach upon the shares of the inheritors ordained by Allah ?

(*iii*) There is no tax on income, which curbs initiative and enterprise. The progressive taxation assumes illegitimacy of the income of the rich. The rising slabs represent taxation with vendetta. Only a proportional tax at a fixed rate (on the pattern of *Zakāt*) is to be levied on the accumulated wealth of the capable taxpayers without any distinction. The capital and the profits are all taken together for the purpose of assessment of the accumulated wealth except that land and equipment and implements of labour and production are exempted from the capital.[15]

14. Iqbal (*Reconstruction*, Lecture VI on "The Principle of Movement . . .") has very well brought out the *equity* underlying the apparent inequality in the shares of the male and the female inheritors.

15. I have the authority of Maulānā Muḥammad Yūsuf Binnorī and Muftī Walī Ḥasan confirming through their *Fatwā* (page 153 of Vol. V of the Register of Dār al-'Iftā', New Town Jāmi' Masjid, Karachi) dated 3 Jumādā I, 1391 that implements of labour and production, which are exempt from *Zakāt*, include mills, factories, ships, aircraft, buses, taxies, etc. Industrial

If these were not exempted the burden of the tax will be shifted on to the consumers of the products.

(*iv*) Only surplus wealth is to be taxed. The surplus is not that which exceeds the satisfaction of the basic needs of life at low level. Rather the surplus is that which is left over when a man has satisfied his needs and desires at a level commensurate with his status in life.

(*v*) The customs duties are all outlawed. The Muslims and the *dhimmīs* have the fundamental right to free import. The nationals of foreign States are to pay duty on a reciprocal basis. This is, as a matter of fact, only a device to discourage the other States from levying the duty. Undoubtedly, the whole trend of Islam is towards free trade and development of economy on an international and not a national basis. Even the distinction between a Muslim and a *Kāfir* is obliterated in respect of economic relationship.[16]

(*vi*) No court fees are permitted, which constitute a denial and a hindrance in the way of justice. The dispensation of justice is the prime duty of the State ; it cannot but be free. Similarly, no revenue stamp or fees of any kind are to be demanded for the transaction of any government business.

(*vii*) Taxation for industrialism is not only unknown but also unthinkable in Islam. Of course, the State is welcome to undertake industrial enterprises either on its own or in partnership with private agencies, but it will do so only as an equal participant

equipment, when used for production and not dealt in as commercial commodity, does not fulfil the condition of "namā'" (growth) for the levy of *Zakāt*. On the other hand, industrial equipment is subject to depreciation. Animals employed in agriculture or let on hire are exempt from *Zakāt* on the authority of the Prophet himself, even though they go on breeding. In short, *Zakāt* is levied on industrial profits and not on industrial equipment.

16. *Vide al-Muḥallā*, VI, 114 (No. 702) :

"لايجوز أخذ زكاة ولاتعشير مما يتجربه تجار المسلمين ، ولامن كافر أصلا ،
تجرفى بلاده أوفى غير بلاده ، الا ان يكونوا صولحوا على ذلک مع الجزية فى
أصل عقدهم ، فتوخذ حينئذ منهم و الا فلا " -

in open competition. Normally it should not resort to "protecting" any State or private industry against fair competition at the expense of the consumers. The sovereignty of the consumer is the essence of fair business provided, of course, that equity in the distribution of income is assured beforehand.

In reviewing the conditions of marketing and commercial exchange down to the middle of the eighth century H. 'Ibn al-Qayyim al-Jawzīyyah has brought out a case which is very much akin to protectionism as we know it today. According to him, it is the worst form of injustice and predation if a particular business man is given the exclusive right to run a shop, involving a guarantee that no one else would be allowed to compete with him in the locality around. 'Ibn al-Qayyim declares it *ḥarām* both for the guarantor and the guarantee. It is remarkable that he condemns it on the ground that "it is a way of expropriation by force and selfish enjoyment of the people's money unlawfully ; *it involves barricading the field which is left wide open by Allah.* It is but meet that Allah will block His blessings away from the one who blocks Allah's bounty and provision away from the people."[17] What else can protectionism be if it is not licensing the local industrialist/s to have exclusive rights of business in a *barricaded field* ?

One cannot help recalling the ordeal of the *fuqahā'* in resisting the innovation of unrecognised taxes imposed by avaricious rulers. The most notable example is that of al-Sarakhsī, the famous *faqīh* of Transoxiana in the fifth century H. He exhorted the people to stop payment of taxes which were not sanctioned by Islam. The atrocious ruler imprisoned him in a well from where he dictated his voluminous books to the pupils sitting on the periphery of the

17. 'Ibn al-Qayyim, *al-Ṭuruq al-Ḥikmiyyah fi's-Siyāsat al-Shar'iyyah* (Egypt : 1317 H.), p. 224.

well. The other example is that of Shaikh Ḥusain b. Muḥsin al-Yamānī, who had to migrate to India because he would not sign the *fatwa* allowing the imposition of a new tax on pearls by Aḥmad Pasha, the Turk *nā'ib* of Luḥya, near Ḥudaidah.[18]

The point is that the imposition of a new tax constitutes a serious violation of the Sharī'ah; it is not just a matter of ingenuity on the part of a minister and his advisers.

18. *Nuzhat al-Khawāṭir*, VIII.

Chapter V

VALUE, PRICE AND WAGES

Utility and Value. The utility of goods and services consists in their satisfaction of the needs and desires of men. The capitalist economy does not tarry to examine the legitimacy of the myriad desires from the viewpoint of morality. It recognises no motive other than purely materialistic and exploits every desire of man for the producer to make profits. Not so with the economy of Islam.

Islam holds supreme the considerations of the social and moral welfare of the community in economic activity and production. There are many desires which are harmful. Instead of allowing for their satisfaction, Islam declares them to be illegitimate and unlawful. He who exploits such desires to increase his profits is a callous anti-social predator. For example, many men have a strong desire for wine. Islam would not allow this desire to be satisfied. Instead it would point out that the desire is harmful :

They ask thee concerning wine and gambling. Say: **"In them is great sin, and some profit,** for men ; **but the sin is greater than the profit" (ii. 219).**

Uncorrupted intelligence would only confirm the verdict of the Qur'ān. Writing on the subject, Taussig says :

Among physiologists the settled conclusion is that though the use of these stimulants [liquors] in the lighter forms may lead to no harm, that of distilled spirits is in most cases bad. It is certain that an immense amount of misery and vice comes from the widespread use of strong liquors ; that the diminutien in their consumption during the last generation or two has brought betterment for mankind; that the world would be a much happier place if drunkenness could be stamped out. What has the economist to say of labour given to the production of things harmful?[1]

By the way, it will be observed that while prohibiting wine to the Muslims, Islam would allow it to the non-Muslims living side by side with the Muslims in an Islamic State. Islam needs no protection behind a curtain. It expects the non-Muslims to be in due course impressed with the superiority of the Islamic way of living in the way of Taussig and also of Toynbee.[2] It is symptomatic of the loss of self-confidence in the present day that the Muslims fear the percolation in their society of the ways of their non-Muslim neighbours. The present-day Muslims would repel with intolerance and exclusiveness where the Muslims of yore attracted with liberal and intimate social intercourse.

Another glaring case is that of opium, ḥashīsh, marijuana and LSD. Islam would see to it that economic activity is subordinated to considerations of the social and moral welfare of the community.

Anyway, before any goods and services acquire "value," their utility has to be approved by our inborn intelligence and inherent moral sense and confirmed by the Sharī'ah. If the *ribā* is outlawed, the services of the bank officials are also devoid of utility and, consequently, of value. The question which puzzled the earlier economists can only be answered straightway on the moral, and not on the economic, plane.

Further, the capitalist economy would concern itself with the production of goods and services to satisfy the needs and desires of a community as a whole. As opposed to it, Islam lays on the

2. Taussig, *Principles of Economics*, I, 20.
2. A. Toynbee, *Civilization on Trial*, p. 207.

community and the State the sacred obligation of attending to the basic needs of each and every individual rather than increasing production for selfish enjoyment by the fortunate ones. Islam recognises no scarcity of goods and services in a community to satisfy the basic needs of each individual. If only the free gifts of Nature were allocated equitably at the primary stage and every member applied his intelligence-labour to them according to his capacity, the production would be enough for the purpose under normal circumstances. The main problem is that of distribution of wealth for the sake of economic and social justice and not the mad pursuit of the purely materialistic motive in swelling the profits of the capitalists.

Price. The approved utility of a thing invests it with an intrinsic value, which is assessed in relation to the factor of scarcity in the market. While the value is intrinsic, the price set on it is relative and constantly subject to varying demand and supply. What is termed "marginal value" is really "marginal vendibility price," i.e. the marginal price at which a particular commodity can be vended in the market at a particular time. It is the essence of social and economic justice that the exchange of goods and services, directly with one another or through the common medium of a commodity such as gold and silver, should go on the natural way subject only to demand and supply in the open market, untampered and unhampered by any artificial restrictions and controls devised by any human agency. The cunning of man would only rig the economic forces to serve the vested interests of the dominant group.

Surplus Value—Where ? In the ultimate analysis, the free gifts of Nature constitute the original wherewithal of economic production. The free goods become economic when some skill and labour are applied to fashioning them. Now if the economic

system ensures that the gifts of Nature remain FREE, the economic goods will be the product of labour alone. Islam ensures that agricultural land, mineral deposits, pasture and standing timber all remain public property and no individual or human agency such as a State turns them into a source of rent.

The application of labour is spread over a long period and through the various stages of production, but the finished product represents only the accumulated labour. The iron deposits being free, the textile machinery represents the skill and labour applied to its turnout. The agricultural land being free, the cotton yarn represents the labour applied to the cultivation and ginning of cotton. The millowner pays the textile worker for his labour and charges for his own management-labour before the finished cloth is offered for sale in the open market under free competition. Where is "surplus value" then ?

Genesis of Exploitation. Undoubtedly, the investment in machinery and the cost of the raw material have to be taken into account in addition to the wages of the workers in a mill. Yet it is a fact that the workers are exploited and the capitalist millowner goes on bagging and piling up undue and illegitimate profits. The rot starts when the gifts of Nature are not FREE, when an individual (or the State itself) charges rent for a piece of agricultural land or a quantity of mineral deposits or a log of timber from another individual. This violation of the character of the FREE goods, which are turned into economic goods at the take-off for development, has far-reaching consequences. It at once splits a community into two classes : a class "possessing" and "owning" an excessive share in the natural resources and another class of those who have no natural resources to apply their labour to. Obviously this latter class is bereft of all bargaining power and constrained to offer its labour to the former class on unfair terms.

If only one had one's share in the free gifts of Nature, one would never undersell one's labour. Naturally one would demand wages higher than the return one expects for one's labour when applied to one's own share of the natural resources.[3]

This is the genesis of all exploitation, which, if not checked at the primary stage of economic development, persists and multiplies from agriculture to industry. The helplessness of the industrial worker arises from his want of a share in the free goods. If the industrial worker is in a position not to allow his labour to be exploited and not to accept anything less than fair wages, and if the industrialist's profits are cut down to proper size by open competition in an "unprotected" market, the phenomenon of surplus value would not occur. The worker gets low unfair wages because he is in the first instance denied his share in the free gifts of Nature and the industrialist fattens upon illegitimate profits—far in excess of a fair return for his management-labour—because of the "protection" assured by the State.

Capitalism. The class which possesses and owns an excessive (i.e. beyond the limit which an individual can put to actual use on his own) share in the natural resources yields place in a capitalist society to capital-owners. The other class which is deprived of its share in the natural resources turns into industrial labour. Obviously the trek from the countryside to the industrial towns is caused by sheer want and distress. In the very nature of things those who offer their labour in distress can have no bargain-

3 Marx is quite true in his gibe that the labourer in the capitalist system is "free in the double sense : that as a freeman he can dispose of his labour-power as his own commodity and that on the other hand, he has no other commodity for sale, *is short of everything necessary for the realisation of his labour-power*." A labourer has every right to a share in the resources of Nature to realise his labour-power. There is no other way of ending his misery and exploitation.

ing power. It is only the privilege of one who can gainfully employ his labour elsewhere to bargain with a new employer, i.e. the industrialist.

It would make all the difference if every member of the society has his own share in the natural resources at the primary stage of development. That is to say, all the traces of feudalism, in which one member is in a position to charge rent for the free gifts of Nature from another member, have to be wiped out before the virus of exploitation is killed in the body of industrialism.

Just as feudalism thrives on the negation of the right of each member to an equitable share in the resources of Nature, similarly capitalism avows a shameless disregard of the fundamentals of equitable distribution of wealth. Capitalism would not admit the obligation of the society to see that the basic needs of each individual are satisfied. Capitalism would produce and go on increasing production, allowing no measure except the purchasing power of the people to regulate the distribution. If some members are denied the opportunity to work or if they are helpless in any other way, capitalism would exploit their misery rather than relieving it. In the developing countries the ruthlessness of capitalism is increased manifold by the umbrella of "protection" held over it by the State. It is a protection against fair competition in production and against fair prices and fair distribution. The results are simply horrible : untold misery in the midst of affluence and increasing want in the wake of increasing production. If carried to logical conclusions, capitalism is overtaken by Nemesis.

There is an explosion which, though it may not rouse the dead conscience, affects the selfish interests of capitalism. Ultimately capitalism sheds a few crocodile tears and puts up a show of concern for the betterment of the lot of the victims of exlpoitation. In reality it only makes a niggardly concession to the threats of violence and destruction coming from those who would not bear its injustices and deprivat ons any longer. Minimum wages, bonuses and shares in the capital and some improvements in the facilities are only props of a rotten system and no signs of a change of heart or the abandonment of the malignant system. The State also saves its policy of protection by resorting to unsuccessful price control when the strain reaches the breaking point. It is a pity that some of our *'ulamā'*, in their zeal to stall socialism, would recommend the same patched-up capitalism as the economic system of Islam.[4]

Labour and Wages. The relationship between an employer and an employee, a millowner and a labourer, takes the form of a contract by free mutual consent of the two parties. Of course, there are moral obligations on either side : fair, generous treatment and prompt payment on the part of the employer and hard work, sincere effort and good performance on the part of the employee. But apart from the moral obligations, the legalities are just concerned with the nature and duration of the work and the amount of the wages. The Islamic *Fiqh* stipulates that the above items be negotiated between the parties and specified beyond doubt in the terms of the contract. Let it be noted that the level of wages is determined only by the free interplay of natural factors just as the level of prices is subject to the free operation of the natural law of supply and demand in the open market. No human agency is to be trusted with the authority to lay down the minimum wages in the same way as price control is outlawed in absolute terms. Of course, both the parties acting as free, responsible agents are the best judge of their interests according to their assessment

4. *Vide* Muftī Muḥammad Shafī'. "Islāmī Niẓām ke Taḥt Ma'āshī Islāḥāt," *al-Balāgh*, Karachi, December 1969.

of the mutual need for exchange of labour with money. The point is that the labourer is not free if he has to sell his labour in distress. It is for the State to relieve him of distress and to invest him with bargaining power by assuring him of the facility to employ his labour in his own share of the free gifts of Nature. This is the curative for the problems of labour. The palliative of fixing a minimum wage assumes injustice, greed and profiteering on the part of the capitalist—evils which are the product of the control of economy by the State. These evils call for decontrol rather than an extension of the controls.

Capitalism sometimes assumes an air of pity and kind concern for natural wages to the labourer. Nobody is deceived by the anxiety to keep the labourer at subsistence level, not to kill the goose that lays the golden egg. This, however, brings out another aspect of the plight of the labourer, who has to depend for his subsistence on the selfish interests of his blood-suckers. This is just because the State disowns responsibility for satisfying the basic needs of its citizens. When the pendulum swung to the other extreme, the communist thinkers argued that the economic goods were the product of labour and labour alone so much so that the capital-owner had no contribution to make to the value of the goods and was not entitled to any return for the same. This is undoubtedly true of the capitalist society where capital represents illegitimate unearned income and the labourer is constrained to sell his labour in distress. This is all the more so in developing countries where industrialism is given State support in the name of nationalism. Otherwise, capital and the instruments of production all represent accumulated labour over a long period and through various stages of production. Also, the millowner has a legitimate claim to adequate reward for his management-labour. The myth has long been exploded that all labour is productive of goods. Rather all labour is valuable which contributes to bringing about satisfactions, which are morally desirable and lawful.

Wages are evaluated according to the productivity of labour and utility of the services of the employee. The personal needs of the labourer-employee for subsistence or comforts need not enter into consideration of the worth of his services. This is because the satisfaction of the needs of the employee is no responsibility of the employer. Rather it is the responsibility of the State, whose function it is to bring about an equitable distribution of the resources of Nature, to regulate the acquisition of wealth, and to institute a system of social security in which the capable and talented members contribute to the welfare of the less capable and incapable members of the society. The State cannot shove this responsibility on to the shoulders of the employer.

It is another common misuderstanding that the price of a product determines the wages of the labourers who work to produce it. Prices find their level in the open market through the operation of demand and supply. Wages are determined by the quality and duration of the work and its value and utility for the society. The value and utility of work and service is not measured by the amount of physical labour involved. Rather the qualities of mind—knowledge, learning, skill and training, planning, direction, execution and supervision—have much greater value and utility than manual and physical labour. In short, work, service and labour find their own level of price (wages) like the commodities in the open market subject to the factor of scarcity.

It does happen on a short term that the wages of the workers turn out to be far above or below the actual price of the finished goods in the market. But in the long run there is always a natural adjustment between the cost of production (including the wages) and the market price of the goods. In the same way there is an adjustment between the earnings of a labourer and the established requirements of a reasonable standard of living, provided the labourer is free from a sense of helplessness and distress. Anyhow, it would be just tinkering with the problem if an external authority like the State intervenes to link wages artificially either with the needs of the labourer for subsistence or with the price of the finished product. It would not contribute to the natural, wholesome and stable growth of the economy, nor would it ensure full justice to the cause of the labourer. It would only help the vested interests in the capitalist-controlled economy to take a new lease of life.

Chapter VI

BANKING AND INSURANCE

(1) *Banking*

The fact is little known that banking services came into vogue early in the Abbasid period. These services answered the need for safe deposit of enormous hoards of wealth, for concealing unlawful income, for guarding against confiscation (*muṣādarah*) by the State on various pretexts (political vendetta, personal jealousy, greed of the rulers and sometimes penalty for corruption), for ease of operation of accounts and money transactions and for remittance of huge sums and their conversion from one currency into another. The Jews earned a reputation for offering these services most efficiently and reliably and the Muslims—both government and the people—were quick to avail themselves of the services of the Jews without any prejudice on religious grounds. It was very much like the medical profession in which the Christians were the most prominent.[1] The restrictions on the employment of the *dhimmīs* (the Christians and the Jews) in government service (because of doubts concerning their loyalties, which unfortunately were confirmed during periods of political and military crises) were relaxed to admit them to the financial and monetary administration of the State. No doubt, the political influence which the Jews acquired through their control of the finances of the State was invariably resented and in course of

1. According to al-Maqdisī, most bankers, dyers, money-changers and tanners in Egypt and Syria were Jews; most medical men and clerks were Christians.

time came to be the subject of angry protests by the public through the vituperations of their chief spokesmen, namely, the poets, and sometimes also through an outburst of frenzied violence.

Unfortunately, a coherent account of the banking practices of those early days has to be reconstructed with the help of casual hints strewn about the annals of political history. It is a painstaking task which the modern Muslims have not yet attempted in a serious and methodical manner. The researches of the Orientalists, particularly of Dr Walter J. Fischel of the Hebrew University, Jerusalem, have unearthed enough material to justify the above assertion that banking practices were well known in the lands of Islam during the Abbasid period. They grew naturally out of the needs of commerce and the administration of finance in that age and were developed at the hands of the Jews. It will be noted that the terms of banking are mostly Arabicised Persian, which is a pointer to the existence of previous Persian usages though perhaps in an embryonic form. The broad outlines of the picture that emerges before us are as follows.

Towards the end of the ninth century C.E. the Muslim Caliphate had changed over entirely to the gold standard, replacing the silver dirham of the previous days. By the same time the maintenance of the prescribed standards of fineness and the quality of gold content and the equivalence of the various currencies had become an important function of the State Treasury. The functionary who specialised in the job was designated *jahbadh* (Arabicised form of the Persian *kahbad*). We first hear of a *jahbadh* during the time of al-Manṣūr (754-75), but it was only in later times that the office and its functions were clearly defined and became a regular feature of the financial administration. A full-fledged *Dīwān al-Jahbadhah* came into being and a *jahbadh* was put in charge of each province. The *jahbadh* was like an authorised bank to collect the revenue of the province allotted to him. Every *jahbadh* had to furnish detailed statements (*khatmāt* = ختمات) to the government. Usually the *jahbadh* was a commercial magnate (*tājir*) who owned capital of his own and was able to advance money to the government when the treasury was empty, which case was not so infrequent. The Jewish *tujjār* were best suited to advance huge sums to the government because they commanded vast capital resources of their own and could also rely on the resources of their coreligionists in the various parts of the Caliphate. These loans, which the governments often resorted to, were negotiated for interest, the usual rate being one dirham per dīnār.[2] The governments also found it expedient to maintain the stability of the office of the *jahbadh* in the same way as the governments guarantee the solvency of the banks today:

The Caliph did not want to dismiss them, in order to uphold the dignity of the office of *jahbadh* in the eyes of the merchants, so that the merchants might be ready to lend their money through the *jahbadh* if necessary. Were a *jahbadh* to be dismissed and another appointed in his place with whom the merchants had not yet had any dealings, the business of the Caliph would come to a standstill.

The Jewish merchants and bankers also came to have huge deposits with them. Hoarding of money had become a passion with the people of that age and they needed someone on whom they could rely to keep and administer their hoardings for them honestly and efficiently. The Jews provided the exact answer to the need. They kept the accounts accurately and scrupulously. Apart from straightforward deposits there were also secret

2. At times the rate fluctuated between 15 and 30, even 50, dirhams to a dīnār. *Ency. of Islam*, "DIRHAM".

deposits, which the high officials would entrust to the merchant bankers while taking care that they were not entered in books. High officials, like the Wazīr Ibn al-Furāt, also had "bribery money" remitted direct to their banker, who would credit it to their account without creating any evidence of the existence of such money. These Jews were famous for "reporting to heirs of the secret deposits received by them from merchants from near and far upon their clients' death. This honesty on their part secured them a good name in every land, and accordingly they prospered."

The accounts were operated by the depositors through cheques (Ar. *ṣakk* from Persian). The banker charged a commission—about one dirham per dīnār—for his services.

The bankers were most serviceable in regard to remittances abroad. *Suftajah* (again a borrowing from Persian), i.e. letter of credit/bill of exchange, was the established means of such transactions. Even the revenue of the provinces was transferred to Baghdad by means of *safātīj* (pl. of *suftajah*). We also hear of special messengers called *fayj* (فيج, also Arabicised Persian) running with letters of credit to and fro. This service was also rendered in consideration of a charge of one dirham per dīnār by the banker.

The above account is based on Fischel's *Jews in the Economic and Political Life of Mediaeval Islam* (London : 1937). It will be observed that the bankers provided real and much-needed services to depositors and business men and charged a legitimate fee or discount for the same. Apart from the incidental immorality involved in helping the corrupt officials to conceal their black money, there could be no objection from the Islamic viewpoint to the growth of the services as such. The Muslims also figure as money-changers (Ar. *ṣairafīyy/ṣarrāf* from which Eng. "shroff") and operators of remittances. But, of course, the Muslims were greatly handicapped in the banking business because of their inability to make advances on interest. That is why they could never be useful to the State, which had to accord a privileged position to the Jews as soon as it came to depend on borrowings. It was the same with the Hindu moneylenders in India under the Muslim rule.

So far the banker did not pay any interest on deposits. On the whole the Muslims have observed more strictly the prohibition against taking interest than against paying interest on loans. It has been observed that the bankers were commercial magnates who traded in goods on their own account. They carried on this business with their own capital and probably also took the risk of investing the deposits of their clients in it for their own profits (not for distribution among the depositors). This practice is, of course, fraudulent and, according to Islam, the gains accruing therefrom are illicit gains. Investment in business should be with the consent of the depositor and on conditions prescribed for the *muḍārabah.*

As the banker prospered in trade and business he attracted more deposits by offering interest than would come to him for safe-keeping only. This is, of course, impossible in Islam. It involves exploitation and usurpation of the full share of the depositor in the actual profits of the enterprise in which the deposits are invested. The banning of interest is to safeguard the larger return of the profits to the depositor and not to deprive him of the smaller return in the form of interest, which is invariably a meagre part of the profits.

If the banker is himself a business man, he is only guilty of misappropriating the legitimate share of the depositor in the profits. Not content with that, the banker started offering loans to industrialists and business men on interest. Thus from an active business man who made unlawful use of the deposits of his clients, he turned into a middleman between the depositor and the business manager. "In modern times there has been a great development of the class of middlemen who intervene between the investors and the active managers. There have been great possibilities of profit for those middlemen, great possibilities of abuse in positions of trust, but also great effectiveness in collecting and investing the savings that underlie the enormous growth in the total capital of modern communities." Islam would not tolerate any practice which does more harm than good. Middlemen are abominable creatures who fatten on the labour of others. The profits of an enterprise legitimately belong to the investor and the manager; no middleman is to be allowed to take an illegitimate share in them. After all, the banker contributes nothing to the capital or management. The whole spirit of Islam is to bring the investor into direct contact with the manager. The effectiveness in collecting the savings is offset by general apathy and loss of active interest in the success of the enterprise on the part of the investor. This undermines the very foundation of a sound and viable economy and renders all development subject to the selfish manipulations of a few gambling speculators.

Saving and investment is a natural habit—almost an instinct—with man, and a capable and reliable manager can always be sure of eager co-operation from big as well as small investors. Take, for example, the case of Mecca, where at the time of the Prophet the majority of the inhabitants were merchants who employed their own capital and/or the capital which others entrusted to their care. Managerial skill was at high premium and much sought after by the investors. The capital was never so shy or timid as to avoid risk. In the words of the author of the article on Mecca in the *Shorter Encyclopaedia of Islam*. "It would be difficult to imagine a society in which capital enjoyed a more active circulation [than in the Meccan society]. . . . The sleeping partnership (*muḍāraba*) was much in favour, especially 'the partnership for the half,' which supposes 50% participation in the profits by the sleeping partners. Thanks to the development of these institutions the humblest sums could be invested, down to a gold dīnār or even a *nashsh* or half dīnār. Such a flexible organisation stimulated even the humblest to take his share in commercial enterprises."

I would not reopen here the question of interest in Islam. Despite all the attempts of the modernists, the question has remained settled beyond any doubt. It will be recalled that "in mediaeval times the acceptance of interest by lenders was prohibited, at least for the Christians (the prohibition was by church law and applied to Christians only, hence the position of the Jews as monylenders). To receive from the borrower more than had been lent him was thought unrighteous. The explanation of this attitude, so different from the present-day acceptance of interest as a matter of course, is probably that during the Middle Ages borrowing was in the main for consumption. When the borrower uses loans for his own gainful operations the bargain between him and the lender for interest seems natural and equitable." This is exactly the line taken by the modernists who would like the Muslims to follow the Christians in declaring commercial interest (as distinguished from usury) as lawful. Suffice it to say that if the loan is used for productive commercial enterprise, then the lender should in fairness have his full share in the profits. In this case the ban on interest is designed to safeguard the legitimate right of the lender. (In the other case when the loan is for consumption, the prohibition of interest aims at saving the borrower from the callousness of the lender.) The injustice lies in the borrower's earning commercial profit and paying the lender a mere pittance by way of interest instead of his full legitimate share in the profit.

It is only the baneful influence of a middleman which demoralises the capital-owner and makes him content with the mere pittance of interest. When he has direct contact with the manager he always aspires to full participation in the fortunes and profits of an enterprise. The growth in the size of the industrial and commercial undertakings is no excuse for putting up with a middleman. If the banker can attract capital with the promise of interest, the manager is in a much better position to collect it with the prospects of "partnership for the half". It is not that the Arabian society knew only of consumption loans ; only no one was so timid and so foolish as to be content with interest, knowing that his capital was employed to produce much larger profits.

Once the banker is entrenched in a position of abuse of financial control, he starts lending not money or capital but *credit*. "Uncovered issue," discounting of Promissory Notes and created deposits are all fraudulent tricks played upon an unwary public. In this particular case credit is only a misnomer for taking chances with the credulity of the customers and introducing the element of gambling in business enterprise. Just see the banker building up loans and creating deposits on reserves in the ratio of 10 to 1 and feeling safe with the holding of legal tender money just about 5% of the demand obligations. The whole business is reduced to speculative gambling, which "saps character and distracts from the sober continuous work on which the common welfare rests". It is now recognised on all hands that "all the real and serious evils of speculation are made greater, or at least made more easily possible, by the willingness of banks to lend funds on call to anyone who will pledge sufficient security." Many a modern economist has now perceived the seamy side of growth piled on growth and has veered round to the view that "the creation of deposits and all that hangs thereby had better be put an end to once for all. The most radical suggestion for change has been that commercial banks should be compelled to keep reserves up to the full amount of their deposits, a reserve of 100 per cent."[3] This is a clear vindication of the position of Islam *vis-a-vis* the speculative gambling on the part of the banker.

It may be mentioned here that some doubts have been cast upon the practice of *suftajah* in the light of the general principles of the Sharī'ah. There can be no objection to a bill of exchange as an instrument of honest transaction and remittance of money.[4] The *fuqahā'* disapprove of any advantage accruing from it over and above the exchange of money. For example, they do not like the *suftajah* being practised deliberately with the intention to save the remittance charges. Later developments have shown that the practice easily lends itself to manipulation for advancing money on interest and "creating credit". This is, of course, prohibited in Islam.

To sum up, the practice of "advancing credit" or "creating deposits" in any form is simply discountenanced in Islam. If the banker is himself a *tājir*—a merchant or an industrialist—he can invest the deposits in business on conditions of *muḍārabah* with the depositors as partners. Otherwise the entire spirit of Islam and the practice of the past centuries are against according recognition to the services of a middleman between the capital-owner and the business manager. It is very doubtful if the bank can be entrusted with such a function under Islamic law.

3. Taussig, *Principles of Economics*, I, 346.
4. Manāẓir 'Aḥsan Gīlānī, *'Islāmi Ma'āshiyāt*, (Hyderabad : 1947), p. 433.

(2) *Insurance*

A co-operative effort at mutual help on the part of a group of similarly placed individuals is an act of virtue and beneficence. Whenever an individual is exposed to a certain mishap in the pursuit of an avocation and liable to pay an indemnity beyond the capacity of a single person, mutual interest in security also demands that the burden of the individual be shared by the group to which he belongs. In the pre-Islamic days the liability of an individual to pay the blood-money was regarded as the liability of the tribe as a whole. Islam set the seal of approval on the practice, which was also beneficial in generating social pressure for moral rectitude. The notable features of the practice of *ma'āqil* serve us as guidelines for arriving at a verdict upon the "insurance business" of our own day.

Firstly, insurance is in essence a co-operative effort for mutual help and security. It should be so designed as to liquidate itself when the objective of collective payment of indemnity for the acts of an individual member of the group is fulfilled. This is a far cry from insurance as an industry founded on the profit motive and run on business and commercial lines. It is the worst form of the callous exploitation of the misery of the helpless common folk. Co-operative effort must of necessity be confined to the group concerned; no business man should have any business to make capital out of it.

Secondly, such co-operative effort at mutual help should not be used as a means of capital formation for purposes of industrialism. There are set rules for the collection and investment of capital in business and industry, which should be followed in a direct and forthright manner.

Thirdly, the case of indemnity and legal financial obligations is to be distinguished from a loss suffered by an individual, which involves no obligation to others. By way of illustration, if a man is killed, it is the killer who is under an obligation to pay the blood-money and it is he who needs the help of the group to fulfil his obligation. The heirs of the one who is killed shall be compensated for their loss on behalf of the killer only.

Now, what is the contribution of an insurance "firm" to the welfare of the community? Shrewdly basing his calculations upon the rate of mortality and other factors involved, the manager collects from, say, a hundred, out of a hundred and five, policy-holders enough money by way of premia to cover payments to the five persons who die before the maturity of their policies. Not only that, he makes commercial profit out of the business. Further, he invests the premia in productive enterprises and keeps the larger part of the profits to himself. Is there any room left for beneficence in the sordid affair? It is precisely because of this that the thought of nationalisation turns before everything else to banking and insurance.

A word about the need for insurance. The need arose in the capitalist society because of the apathy of the State to public welfare in the name of freedom of competition. In Islam the primary function of the State is to enforce equity in acquisition and beneficence in distribution with a view to relieving each and every member of the society of want and insecurity. Insurance against old age, unemployment and sickness is an essential function of the State. The *Zakāt* fund is earmarked for many more such items. Nothing is as sure as death. Apart from the indemnity provided for in case of injury or death caused by violence, natural death is taken as a matter of course and adequate support for the survivors regarded as the collective responsibility of the society and the State.

There remain only a few cases in which co-operative effort at mutual help is called forth from the groups concerned. In regard to accidents on the road, the errant driver is liable to pay an indemnity, which, like blood-money, is often beyond his personal capacity. It may quite justifiably be shifted on to the *'āqilah* or the entire group of the car drivers. Each car driver would make his contribution to a pool, which will be utilised to pay compensation to the sufferers. The pool is to be administered by a public body, preferably a government agency, on a strictly self-liquidating basis. If there is an accident the victim is compensated ; if there is no accident nobody profits thereby. It is quite possible that the accumulated surplus be invested in productive avenues and the premium reduced in proportion to the profits assured. Even in the hands of the public body or the State agency it is not going to be a business concern or a subsidiary of industrialism.

Similarly, accidents of fire and loss or damage caused in other ways to shops and business houses and goods în transport by sea or otherwise may be covered by contribtions from the group concerned. Though the dealings of business houses and shipping and transport companies with the clients are on the basis of trust (*'amānat*),[5] the managers would very much like to promote business by assurance of compensation. It must be remembered that it is the managers who take goods on trust ; only they can assure of compensation if they so like. It is not for any speculator outside to exploit the situation for illegitimate profits.

From the viewpoint of Islamic *Fiqh*, insurance can only be classed under *ḍamān* (warrant) which is governed by two essential conditions. Firstly, the guarantor can only take upon himself a

5. The Pious Caliphs decided to indemnify the craftsmen for loss of, or damage to, their clients' material because, in the words of 'Alī, the people generally would not behave righteously and discharge their obligations faithfully without the fear of such indemnity (*vide* al-Shātibī, *al-'I'tiṣām*).

liability which has fallen or may possibly fall upon a person. Secondly, the guarantor is prohibited from charging any fee or taking any money in return for the guarantee. If we take the insurance company as the guarantor, it cannot be said to assume any legal liability of the insured person. Moreover, it offers the guarantee in consideration of a premium, which is enough to turn the guarantee into speculative business.

Lastly, it is only characteristic of the profit motive predominant in the present age that the Muslims are turning away from their own institution of *waqf* to insurance for the promotion of social welfare. In its golden days the Muslim society prided itself on *waqfs* for defraying the marriage expenses of the daughters of poor parents, for helping the needy students and even for making good the loss of utensils by domestic servants so as to protect them from the rage of ill-tempered masters. The institution of the *waqf* is the best embodiment of the spirit of co-operation and mutual help for social amelioration on the part of the God-fearing rich. It contributes at the same time to material welfare as well as social solidarity far more than insurance by callous, avaricious, calculating magnates, whose gains have become almost monopolistic. A similar manifestation of the profit motive is the organisation of charity through sale of tickets for entertainment.

Chapter VII

PRIORITIES AND PRINCIPLES OF PLANNING

There is no *laissez-faire* in Islam. The government has to regulate distribution and production of wealth in many ways. It has also to stimulate agriculture, commerce and industry by partaking in a bold way in those activities without monopolising them.

There is, however, a set order of priorities and the top place in it is assigned to the regulation of distribution and planning for the satisfaction of the basic needs of each and every individual member of the society. In the manner of the tribe of 'Ash'ar (chap. IV, note 13 above), whatever be the gross national wealth it is to be shared with the poor and the needy. It is, therefore, the first and the foremost responsibility of the State to see that the system of *Zakāt* and all the ancillary measures designed to "take the surplus from the rich and distribute it among the poor" function effectively and in a spirit of devotion to Allah.

Secondly, in order to set the course of productive activity, the State has to observe and maintain equity in the distribution of the resources of Nature. The State is to employ all means at its disposal to correct any imbalance in the possession of the resources of Nature, which might result from violation and neglect of the injunctions of the Sharī'ah from time to time. Further, no idle possession of the resources of Nature is to be condoned in any case. Full use of agricultural land by the owner is to be enforced and no owner is to be allowed to charge rent from a fellow human being.

Thirdly, public property—mines, forests, *saib al-bahr*—is to be managed by the State in the best way that ensures maximum output and at the same time preserves the FREE character of the endowments of Nature.

Fourthly, the public utility services which yield profits, such as railways, posts and telegraphs, gas, electricity and water supply, are to be managed by the State or by an agency approved by the State, guided only by considerations of efficient administration and best service at the cheapest rates. The government is not to turn the public utility services into a means of augmenting the revenue of the treasury. When there is a genuine need, the government can very well expand its revenue by taxing the rich in a direct and forthright manner.

Fifthly, the non-profitable public services, such as roads, wells, *musāfirkhānahs*, parks and assembly halls, are to be provided with State funds augmented by contributions from the philanthropists and also by taxation, if necessary. Many of these items fall under the heads of expenditure specified for the *Zakāt* fund.

It will be seen that the development of mines, forests, water and power resources, iron and steel and arms manufacturing industries, falls in the government sector. For all projects which yield profits the State is to depend for necessary resources on borrowings from the public on the basis of partnership and sharing of the profits. As for the industries which form part of the defence establishment, direct taxtion can always be resorted to according to the needs of the situation. Again, such transport and communication projects as yield profits are to be financed with borrowings on the basis of partnership. As there would be no competition, it would be the duty of the government to see that the profits are kept within reasonable limits. Government control and the elimination of competition are designed only to reduce running costs in the public interest. It is immoral on the part of the government to use its power and privilege to make monopolistic gains or to tax the common people indirectly for replenishing the exchequer thereby. It would also be desirable to plan in such a manner that the borrowed capital is paid off in course of time and ultimately the service is run on a no-profit-no-loss basis. Whatever transport and other services are left in private hands, the government is to see that they are run on a healthy competitive basis.

Such projects as yield no profits are to be financed with State funds, which are supplemented with direct taxation according to the easy tax-paying capacity of the people at the stage of prosperity reached by the society at the time. Education, medical facilities and all the social services are to be developed in the same way.

In regard to private commerce and industry it is the duty of the State to have an elaborate and effective system of *ḥisbah*, i.e. on the spot checking of weights and measures, quality of commodities offered for sale, proper gradation, honesty in dealings, and the observance of modesty and courtesy in salesmanship and in the general behaviour of the people. Of course, the government has also the responsibility to break cartels, monopolies, hoarding and corner-market. Apart from legal and administrative measures, the best way is to arrange supplies of abundant cheap goods into the market. 'Umar did it during the days of famine in Medina. The Government of Sweden is trying the method successfully in our own time ; it enters the field of imports and also of production to curb profiteering, restore conditions of healthy competition and bring down the prices to the natural level.

It is only when distribution has been planned in the above way that the State is geared to planning for increased production. By way of a simile, canals have to be constructed and pipelines laid before the water is released to rush in. The State is to give a fillip to economic activity by partaking in it, by setting an example on the same terms and conditions as are admissible to the public. It is a general characteristic of Islamic polity that the State is subject to the same code of law and morality as the public. 'Umar was always anxious that the State land was brought under the plough. Similarly, he would not allow State funds to lie idle; he would invest them in trade and commerce as any capital-owner would do. But the State would always enter the open market to compete on equal terms. The State would never use its authority to infringe upon the sovereignty of the consumer, which is to be respected once equity in the distribution of income is assured. It is only to guard against any possible misuse of State authority that government functionaries are barred from partaking in agriculture or business activity on their own account.[1]

No doubt, the State has the responsibility to promote industrialism. It can take the initiative in many ways but not in the way of cornering the consumers within a walled protected market for a few magnates to fleece them in the name of nationalism. There are two elements essential for a real and stable growth of industry accompanied by an equitable distribution of the prosperity resulting from it. First, the immaterial equipment and technical knowledge. This can be acquired only in the way all knowledge and skill is acquired. There is no short cut to it

1. 'Umar administered a strong rebuke to 'Amr b. al-'Āṣ, the governor of Egypt, on this count. True to his wont, he also confiscated part of the questionable income (al-Balādhurī, *Futūḥ*, chap. on *Miṣr*).

The government servants are not allowed even to accept gifts from the people. *Vide* the words of the Prophet ('Abū Dāwūd, *Sunan*, No. 2946):

"ألا جلس فى بيت امه أوأبيه فينظر أيهدى له أم لا"

and no substitute for it in nationalism and protectionism. Of course, technical hands may be engaged from outside provided it is economical to do so. The second element is the capital resources, which, if needed, can be augmented from outside on the basis of partnership and sharing of the profits. This is possible only when there is mutual confidence and goodwill among the nations without that hatred of the foreigner which is the essence of nationalism. The other way is that of getting loans from abroad on payment of interest. Most of the developing countries have become addicted to it and are unable to think beyond it. Some effort is made to argue the admissibility in Islamic ***Fiqh*** of the Muslims taking loans from non-Muslims on interest. Anyway, the developing countries have now had enough experience of foreign loans to warrant a thorough re-assessment of their economic benefits and political implications. Already there is noticeable the stress on self-reliance, which marks the realisation of the harmful effects of foreign aid in the economic and political enslavement of the receiving countries.

Protectionism. Protectionism is only an offshoot of nationalism, "the Western ideological disease,"[2] which is repugnant to Islam.[3] The gain of the common man lies in his acquisition of the best quality products at the cheapest price. This is possible only when full play is allowed to the comparative advantage and the efficiency of labour in the various parts of the world. The comparative advantage of one part of the world becomes the advantage of the entire people of the world when exchange is free from all restrictions and uninhibited by any prejudice, national or reli-

2. Toynbee, ***Civilization on Trial***, p. 83.

3. To quote Professor Gibb: "... it may seem strange that the *'ulamā'* should not have been outspoken in their condemnation of nationalism and should even appear to accept it as a legitimate political aspiration" (*Modern Trends in Islam* [University of Chicago Press, 1947], p. 116).

gious. The anomaly of the basic philosophy of protectionism is fully exposed when double standards are applied to economic policies on the national and the international plane. Taussig's description of the same is graphic indeed:

> Perhaps the ancient association of foreigner with enemy still lingers. People do not worry when New England buys coal from Pennsylvania: but when coal is bought from Nova Scotia, dire consequences are supposed to ensue. Half a century ago (more or less) the region which is now British Columbia was claimed by the United States to be part of its territory. Had the Oregon question been settled at that time in accord with the American claims, no one would have questioned that the resources of British Columbia in lumber, coal, and fisheries were of advantage to Americans. But once a border line is drawn, the situation is supposed to change: and that which would have brought us gain in the way of more abundant and cheaper supplies is fraught with peril precisely because these supplies came from a foreigner.[4]

The "crafty and insidious animal called the statesman or politician" generates nationalism and the robber barons pounce upon the unreasonable hatred of the foreigner to protect *themselves* against all foreign competition, of course, at the expense of the vast multitude of their own countrymen. Protectionism soon becomes a vested interest of the political and financial wizards, entailing a crushing burden upon the common people. Experience has shown that it is impossible to keep protective duties within moderate limits or as a temporary measure. As time passes on, protectionism is more and more entrenched. By and large, protectionism is the root cause of inflation. It is also responsible for creating conditions which sap the morals of all those engaged in economic activity. Smuggling, black-marketing, adulteration and profiteering have become the order of the day in all the countries which

4. Taussig, *Principles of Economics*, I, 510.

have sought development through protectionism. There is general lamentation over the sudden fall in moral standards as a concomitant of industrial development. The hypocritical moralist and the professional preacher harangue on the virtue of honesty as if moral delinquency were the cause of corruption and exploitation in economics. The truth is the other way round ; it is protectionism which sets the train of callous exploitation and corrupts the morals of all industrialists and business men. Business morals cannot be restored to purity so long as protectionism whips up the greed of the business man. Moral health is dependent on healthy ways of economic activity.

A protected industry is no fair business proposition; it is at bottom supported by taxes extorted from the general body of consumers in the form of artificial prices. Only a fraction of these taxes goes into the pockets of the working men. The industrialist exploits the situation only to swell his ill-gotten profits. If it were only a magic way of creating job opportunities for the unemployed, the general body of consumers would not bleed to death from protectionism.

In any case, protectionism initiates a process of robbing Peter to pay Paul ; Peter is the general body of consumers and Paul the protected industrialist. Who gains if the money remains within the country ?—Of course, the one who amasses it in his possession. The common man loses the larger part of his hard-earned meagre money income for nothing. If imports were free he would have got the full worth of his money, which would have done justice to him as well as to the producer. Exchange, be it commodity for commodity or commodity for gold, is always to the mutual advantage, bringing a just and adequate reward for both the buyer and the seller within the same political unit as well as between different units.

Islam is jealous of political sovereignty for the Muslims. But it would keep the political borders open for trade, commerce and industrial co-operation with all the Muslim and the non-Muslim countries of the world so long as economics does not conflict with defence organisation. It will be noted that there is no room in Islam for customs barriers, restrictive tariffs or exchange control.

The State is there only to guard the free play of the natural economic forces, including the unrestricted flow of goods and services. All this is done in the cosmopolitan spirit of Islam, which repels nationalism and protectionism alike. On the testimony of Taussig, "The protectionist movement is explicable on various grounds. The growth of nationalist feeling was one important cause. Protection seems, to most people, a 'national' policy, and in fact is so, in the sense of causing exchanges to be made within a country rather than between countries. The principle of free trade has a certain cosmopolitan flavour, and assumes as well as promotes a spirit of peace and goodwill among the nations. Another cause was the admitted need of a thoro reconstruction of economic theory. This promoted skepticism as to free trade, which was one of the cardinal doctrines of the older school; altho no part of the system of the older economists has stood the test of time and criticism better than their reasoning about international trade." [5]

Under the present pattern of national economies the real advantage of international trade is lost to the people at large. The internal trade thrives in conditions of freedom for the various parts of a country to exploit ungrudged the comparative advantage accruing to them in particular fields of economic

5. Ibid., I, 540-1.

activity. Similarly, international trade would be a mere exercise in wasteful exchange if it were not based on the recognition of the comparative advantage and the effectiveness of labour in respect of particular products in different countries. In controlled economies—controlled in the name of industrialism and nationalism—this real advantage is lost to the common people, who have to pay an incompetitive extortionist price for protected local products. The State, in alliance with big business, diverts international trade to promote the monopolistic ownership of capital goods by a few industrial magnates. Factories and industrial plants set up in this way, far from being symbols of economic prosperity, are just engines of oppression against the common people as much as against the workers.

The centrifugal, fissiparous and secessionist tendencies which have plagued the developing countries in recent times are fostered a good deal by protectionism.[6] When comparative advantage in economic production is grudged, each part of a country is prone to limit exchanges within its own borders. It has become patent to prop up protectionism with foreign aid ; hence the insistence of each part of a country to ensure for itself the largest share of it. As foreign aid is seldom without strings, industrialism and protectionism soon result in economic bondage and the virtual strangling of the political independence of the aid-receiving country. Before our eyes, the game is being played by the developed countries in all parts of underdeveloped Asia and Africa.

Self-sufficiency is another anomaly in a world knit together

6. The first manifestation of such tendencies is inevitably the language controversy. The denial of superior technical skill and comparative advantage in economics projects itself into the field of knowledge and learning. Each part of a country tends to boost its language—often a mere spoken dialect—into a symbol of separate identity and to give protection to it.

with highly improved means of communication. Just imagine every man trying to be self-sufficient in respect of all his needs. National States trying to be self-sufficient in all respects is as absurd and unnatural as individuals trying to do the same. The ideal should be for an individual as well as a country *to produce something to advantage, which the others would like to exchange for their own products.* There is nothing in Islam to exalt uneconomic self-sufficiency as a fad; on the other hand, there is a good deal to exhort the people to increased skilful and advantageous production and free exchange. Of course, self-sufficiency becomes a necessity when in an emergency a country is surrounded by hostile powers and when others would seek to pressurise it through economic boycott.

The true asset of a nation is its immaterial equipment, which creates its own capital. The real way to develop the economy of a country is to increase the technical know-how of its people through educative methods and to introduce a pattern of society and government which would reduce social barriers and encourage private enterprise, creative thinking and scientific invention Much more than intellectual attainments and elaborate technical training, a progressive nation needs accumulated moral qualities. "Habits of industry, truthfulness, honesty, sobriety, of consideration for others, of care for the common good—all these are of slow growth, and rest on repeated example and precept."[7] Experience has proved that protectionism causes a sharp moral decline.

It is a hard and long way, indeed, to learn how to produce a thing to advantage. There is only one way of learning an art and a skill, which is apprenticeship. An unskilled people should, in the first instance, seek opportunities of apprenticeship with the skilled peoples of the world. Industrial establishments are the

7. Taussig, op. cit., I, 95.

best place for learning technical knowledge and skill. The way to capital formation is through sharing the profits in a proportionate and equitable manner. Such profits offer a much healthier and stronger incentive to saving and investment than the bait of a small fixed interest. The imposition of an incompetitive extortionist price for protected local products is unfair and unbusinesslike and quite justifiably leaves behind a sense of deprivation and loss in the common man. When the activity of the industrialist is governed by awkwardly selfish motives of greedy exploitation, the common man should not be forced to tighten the belt for no palpable gain to himself. He would, of course, come forward willingly and enthusiastically to contribute to economic development if he were made a partner in it with all the risks and gains attending upon it. Foreign capital can also be invited on the basis of working partnership, in which case not only the resources but also the superior skill of an advanced people would come into full play. This would offer the best opportunity of apprenticeship, of learning in a spirit of comradeship. Of course, there should be no grudge of a foreigner earning a legitimate return for his skill and investment. This is possible only in an atmosphere of goodwill and mutual confidence between the nations concerned. If the international atmosphere today is polluted with aggressive nationalism and super power politics, then there is no alternative to self-reliance for an independent, self-respecting people. The present pattern of foreign aid only sets agoing a cycle of increasing financial burden, which few developing countries have been able to cast off in a lifetime. It is now fully exposed that the motive behind foreign aid is not so much the economic development as the political strangulation of the newly independent developing countries of Asia and Africa. Perhaps China is the only example of an underdeveloped country spurning foreign aid to escape political strangulation and emerging as a developed country in its own right. Egypt and some other countries of the Middle East are outstanding examples of victims of naked attempts at political strangulation through the lever of aid by all and sundry. Pakistan has had the worst experience of its kind during the last two years of natural calamity and political crisis. There has been a case of even humanitarian aid being contaminated and pressed with unfriendly political motives. This experience has been a blessing in disguise inasmuch as it has forced self-reliance on our thoughts. Let us hope that self-reliance would emerge as the bed-rock of the new pattern of our economy in the near future.

The Myth of Equality. As an extreme reaction to the crushing *inequity* in the appropriation of the free gifts of Nature and the reward for labour, there has emerged the demand for *equality* in the distribution of wealth. The demand is merely sentimental, almost childish. As soon as its protagonists come to brass tacks they find it impracticable and deceptive like a mirage. They would themselves rule out mathematical equality as merely Utopian, if not fantastic. Coming down to the communist dictum "From each according to his capacity and to each according to his need," that also remains a pious wish. Coupled as it is with the abolition of private property it calls for an amoral merciless dictatorship to determine for each what he is capable of and what he needs for life. As each one loses the incentive to work and the sense of justice in the inequality of reward, the dictatorship has to force each one to yield according to his predetermined capacity and to accept without demur what is doled out for his predetermined needs of life. The first part of the dictum is a tacit avowal of the difference in the capacity of each, which is a stark fact of life as it is. There is no use questioning the fact; let us accept it with a good heart, without any malice or grudge. This can be achieved only if each one of us is convinced of the innate limitations of his capacity through full freedom and opportunity to develop and prove it at his initiative. Differences in the capacity—mental, temperamental and physical—of each one of us are patent and quite palpable. But one would never be convinced of the design of God or, let us say, the dispensation of Nature without testing it for one's self. It is in the nature of man to bring out the best in him prompted by the hope of adequate reward in proportion to his output. He would at the same time resent and spurn the imposition upon him of the judgment—even if it be true—of an external authority in regard to his capacity for work.

Further, there can only be a general agreement on the basic needs of life. As for the amenities and comforts over and above the basic needs, the only limitation of them willingly acceptable to a man is that of his own efforts towards their attainment without let or hindrance. The determination of one's share in amenities and comforts by an external authority shall always be irritating and unconvincing. The practice of communism so far is characterised by two features: in regard to production one is forced to work without sufficient incentive; in regard to distribution there is as much disparity between the highest and the lowest as anywhere else. It will always remain a grand superstition to hope that each man would put in his best willingly and share the joint product with the rest equally while the State dissolves itself into thin air. Such a system is against the design of God and beyond the ingenuity of man.

Islam urges upon us to accept inequality in material riches as a fact of life in accord with the wisdom of Allah:

Is it they who would portion out the Mercy of thy Lord? It is We Who portion out between them their livelihood in the life of this world: and We raise some of them above others in ranks, so that some may command work from others (xliii. 32).

And in no wise covet those things in which Allah hath bestowed His gifts more freely on some of you than on others (iv. 32).

Allah has bestowed His gifts of sustenance more freely on some of you than on others (xvi. 71).

It is He Who hath made you (His) agents, inheritors of the earth: He hath raised you in ranks, some above others: that He may try you in the gifts He hath given you (vi. 165).

Having accepted *inequality* with a good grace, man is set on the quest for *equity* in economic relationship. This is ensured by a just and adequate reward for one's efforts, which actualise the varying capacities of each. How could the variation in the capacities of each one of us be known and measured precisely unless each had an equal opportunity to put in the best of his effort? If one is to be convinced of the limitations of his capacity, the onus of proving the capacity should rest on one's self.

Further, it is fallacious to assume that *musāwāt* (مساواة), i.e. equality in material wealth, is indispensable or constitutes the only factor in bringing about a happy relationship between man and man. The attitude towards fellow human beings is a matter of psychology, a quality of heart, a matter of inner belief rather than of pure economics. The cornerstone of a fruitful and pleasurable human relationship is *mu'āsāt* (مؤاساة) and not *musāwāt* in the sense of equality in material wealth. *Mu'āsāt* signifies sharing the joys and sorrows of others and dedication of one's resources and efforts to the betterment of the lot of the society. It is an effective antidote to economic inequality and prevents any feeling of hatred or jealousy of the rich by the poor. Islam takes the sting out of economic inequality, making it fully compatible with perfect social equality. Also the economic activity is characterised by a spirit of co-operation, fair mutual exchange and wholesome effort at excellence for the collective good of the people rather than cut-throat competition leading to monopolistic control of economic life by a few magnates.

THE END

INDEX